Studies on the Chinese Market Economy Series

The Chinese Securities Market

Chief editors:
Gao Shangquan *and* Chi Fulin
Written by:
Zhu Huayou

FOREIGN LANGUAGES PRESS   BEIJING

First Edition 1996

The project is aided by
Hainan (China) Foundation for Reform and Development Research.

ISBN 7-119-01491-9
© Foreign Languages Press, Beijing, China, 1996
Published by Foreign Languages Press
24 Baiwanzhuang Road, Beijing 100037, China
Distributed by China International Book Trading Corporation
35 Chegongzhuang Xilu, Beijing 100044, China
P.O. Box 399, Beijing, China
Printed in the People's Republic of China

Editors' Note

Since China started issuing state treasury bonds in 1981, its securities market has been booming. It has not only established its position in the world's stock business, but has also developed its own unique features. China's securities market has played an important role in raising funds for the country's socialist economic construction by helping push the enterprises into the market, promoting the establishment of a modern enterprise system, opening up new channels for the import of foreign capital. The Chinese stock market is in sync with both the Chinese and the international market.

China's securities market is a newly emerging market that has developed rapidly. And, being such a young and fast-growing market, it has its share of problems. It is extremely important for the sound development of China's securities market to study the characteristics and problems in its development and raise policy suggestions for its future improvement.

To further develop and refine China's securities market, in 1992 the China (Hainan) Institute for Reform and Development established a special group to study the country's securities market. The group has conducted a systematic study of the country's securities market and produced a comprehensive report. In April 1993, the institute co-sponsored, along with the UN Development Program (UNDP), an international seminar on the development of China's securities market. Noted scholars in China and experts on securities business from UNDP, the World Bank, Japan, Singapore, the Republic of Korea and Thailand held extensive discussions on major issues regarding the development and improvement of China's securities market. They proposed a number of important theories and policy suggestions. This book presents their findings and also the report produced by the China (Hainan) Institute of Reform and Development. References are made to the related materials and speeches presented at the seminar as well as research achievements made by experts over recent years on the securities business.

Approaching the question from six different angles, this book addresses important issues related to the development of China's securities market. It does not intend to provide the sole answer but aims at presenting readers the valuable views of both Chinese and overseas experts in a comprehensive and systematic manner.

Contents

Chapter 1
Development of China's Securities Market and the Problems It Faces

Section 1 China's Securities Market: Development, Status Quo and Problems

1. Various Stages of Development of China's Securities Market: Debut, Development, Concentrated Trading and Accelerated Development.

Beginning in 1949, China adopted the system of planned economy. In the 1980s, it began to loosen the shackles of this three-decade-long economic strategy and enter the era of the socialist market economy.

The development of China's securities market can be divided into the following four stages:

(1) Securities Market Debut (1981-88): At this stage, government bonds first appeared. They carried the stigma of the planned economy and the market for government bonds was not standard. A small number of enterprises also began to raise funds through the market.

In the early days of the People's Republic, China also issued government bonds. However, this practice was interrupted after 1958. For quite many years, the government had relied on collection of taxes and profits turned in by state-owned enterprises for its revenues. The restructuring of the economic system, launched in 1979, brought about a change in the pattern of national income distribution; the allocation of funds in society tended to be more scattered; and the amount of funds amassed by the government went down relatively. To cope with the changed situation, the government began to issue bonds to raise funds (mainly for economic construction).

The bonds issued by the government in 1981-88 were long-term state treasury bonds. The bonds issued before 1985 had a term of 10 years and those issued after 1985 had a term of five years. The buyers were state-owned and collective enterprises, industrial administrative departments and local governments, institutions, urban and rural individuals, as well as private industrial and commercial business owners and private enterprises. For state treasury bonds issued before 1985, the annual interest rates were 4 percent for collectives and 8 percent for individuals. In 1985, they were raised to 5 and 9 percent respectively, while in 1986, they were again increased to 6 and 10 percent.

The distribution of government bonds was mainly conducted by purchases of assigned quotas, that is, after the Ministry of Finance decided the total amount of the issues, it was up to the financial departments at various levels to determine the quotas for different units or collectives in proportion to their extra-budgetary funds or post-tax profits; banks at various levels and their affiliated offices served to collect the funds and turn them in to the state treasury. For individual buyers, the quotas were also decided by the financial departments in proportion to the people's incomes in the urban and rural areas; the units in which the individuals were employed and the banks in which they opened accounts took the responsibility to collect the funds and turn them in to the state treasury.

During this period, since it still carried the stigma of the planned economy, the market for government bonds was far from being perfect and its performance was far from being standard. First, the distribution of government bonds was done through administrative assignment of quotas. Second, the bonds issued were not allowed to be transferred and circulated on the market. Third, the interest rates for bonds issued to enterprises and individuals differed; the interest rates for bonds purchased by enterprises were lower than the interest rates for bank savings, and the low interest rates made it impossible for enterprises to be enthusiastic in purchasing the bonds. Therefore, the market for government bonds at this stage could only be described as "the debut" of the securities market in China.

At this stage, some enterprises also began to issue their own bonds to raise funds. Although a few enterprises issued bonds to society, most of them, however, issued bonds to their own workers and staff. It was particularly so for rural enterprises which adopted the method of "exchanging funds for jobs," that is, acquiring a job by investing a certain amount of money in an enterprise. In 1989, some key enterprises in the electric power and metallurgical industries issued so-called key enterprise bonds. The buyers were limited to other enterprises, and the enterprises that issued bonds more often than not paid dividends to the bond holders in the form of their own products. This practice of exchanging funds with job opportunities or products that were covered by state unified allotment indicated the nonmarketable character of the bonds and showed that the country's securities market was still in a beginning stage.

At this stage, however, a few enterprises took the lead to issue shares to procure funds. These pioneers included the Shenzhen Bao'an Joint Investment Co., Shanghai Feile Audio Equipment Co. and Yanzhong Industrial Co., as well as Beijing Tianqiao Co. Ltd. After 1986, some state-owned enterprises began to shift to the shareholding system and issued shares openly; these included the Shanghai Vacuum Electronic Device Co. Ltd., Feile Co. Ltd., Shenyang Jinbei (Gold Cup) Motor Vehicle Co. Ltd. and Shenzhen Development Bank. Apart from a few of them, the majority issued shares within themselves or at the most within the industries. Moreover, the shares issued were not standard: some were shares and others were actually bonds.

During this period experiments were conducted in Shenyang and Shanghai on the transfer of enterprise bonds or shares. In August 1986, Shenyang's municipal investment company experimented in enterprise bond transfers, mortgages and certification. In September the same year, the Jing'an Department of Shanghai Trust and Investment Company, affiliated with the Industrial and Commercial Bank of China, started to provide commissioned services in the purchasing and selling of shares. All this provided valuable experience for the establishment of secondary securities markets.

The securities market began to take shape in China during this first stage: state treasury bonds were issued, enterprise bonds, financial bonds and shares all made their appearance. Experiments were conducted in the establishment of secondary markets for shares and other securities. However, bonds issued during this period not only were small in amount, they were not standard, either.

(2) Securities Market Development (1988-90): Spurred on by the development of secondary markets for state treasury bonds, the expansion of securities market was greatly accelerated.

From 1981 to 1988, the amount of state treasury bonds issued amounted to 45.5 billion yuan. But, the bonds did not enjoy a good reputation as they were distributed through quotas set by administrative means and were not allowed to freely circulate. The market for enterprise bonds also developed during this period. Compared with the period prior to 1987, bonds and securities issued during this period were mainly geared towards society, while those issued before 1987 were mainly aimed at raising funds within the enterprises themselves. Moreover, bonds and securities issued in this period were more regular. In March 1987, the State Council promulgated Provisions on the Issue of Enterprise Bonds, with the purpose of making the issue of enterprise bonds standard. In addition, during this period the issue of enterprise bonds was no longer limited to small enterprises and rural ones: state-owned enterprises, collective enterprises with good economic returns, as well as Sino-foreign joint ventures also entered the securities market to raise funds through issuing bonds. For instance, 100 large and medium-sized enterprises obtained approval from the People's Bank of China to issue bonds totalling 3 billion yuan in value. In the same year, enterprises in Shanghai issued 1.446 billion yuan worth enterprise bonds; they included such large enterprises as the Jinshan Petrochemical Works, Shanghai Chloric Soda General Plant and Shanghai Petrochemical Works. Large enterprises in other cities also came to the securities market to raise funds, including the Wuhan Iron and Steel Co., Handan Iron and Steel Co. and Jinbei (Gold Cup)

Motor Vehicle Co. Ltd. This situation indicated that state-owned large and medium-sized enterprises no longer relied exclusively on financial allocations and loans from state banks, but turned to the monetary market for funds.

During this period, the securities market, particularly the trading or secondary market, developed fairly rapidly. It was particularly so in Shanghai and Shenzhen as the State Council decided to allow the two cities to experiment in the trading of shares. Shanghai first issued shares in 1984 and tried out trading of shares issued by two enterprises in 1986. By 1990, the shares of seven joint-stock companies were listed. Of the more than 240 million yuan of capital stock raised, funds contributed by individuals totalled 66 million yuan. Shares traded were mainly those held by individuals. Prior to the establishment of the Shanghai Stock Exchange in 1990, the total turnover was less than 100 million yuan.

The Shenzhen Stock Exchange came into being later than the Shanghai Stock Exchange, but its development was very rapid. In 1987, the Shenzhen Development Bank took the lead in issuing shares, and the lucrative returns from investment in shares in the ensuing two years greatly inspired the local investors. Five share-holding enterprises followed suit to trade their shares in the market. Consequently, the volume of shares traded increased rapidly: in 1988 it was merely 4 million yuan; in 1989 it increased to 23 million yuan; and by 1990 it jumped to 1.76 billion yuan.

At this time, the security transactions in Shenzhen and Shanghai were all over-the-counter deals. While the demand for shares sharply increased, the development of a new-issue market, however, was at a standstill. Furthermore, the contradiction between the supply and demand caused stock price hikes. To put a brake on this trend, the two cities adopted a measure to limit the share prices, which led to rampant off-the-books deals.

During this period, the issue of monetary bonds was also expanded. In 1985, all commercial banks issued monetary bonds. After 1988, other monetary organizations joined the ranks.

(3) Unified and Concentrated Over-the-Counter Trading (1990-91): This stage was marked by the establishment of the

Shanghai Stock Exchange and the dawning of systematic computer trading.

In the early period after its establishment, the Shanghai Stock Exchange mainly offered trading in bonds; later, it offered trading in both bonds and shares. Since then, transactions on shares must be conducted within the exchange; the same is true for transactions on bonds with a value over 2,000 yuan. At the onset, the exchange traded in 31 varieties of shares and bonds (eight varieties of shares). By 1991, the number reached 39, with a total annual turnover of 9.1 billion yuan, of which 7.5 billion yuan were in bonds and 1.6 billion yuan in shares.

The establishment of the Shanghai Stock Exchange not only marked the beginning of concentrated trading of shares and bonds, but also signified the application of computers in stock trading, thus greatly raising efficiency and fundamentally putting an end to all off-the-books trading.

The Shenzhen Stock Exchange was formally opened in July 1991 after a year's preparation and trial operation. Six varieties of shares were traded in 1991, with a total annual turnover of 3.555 billion yuan. The means and procedures of trading in the Shenzhen Stock Exchange were the same as in the Shanghai Stock Exchange.

Soon after the Shanghai Stock Exchange started operation, another concentrated over-the-counter market — the National Securities Trading Automated Quotation System (STAQ) was launched on December 5, 1990. It constituted a market for concentrated over-the-counter trading in securities through computer networks, which linked up securities agencies scattered all over the country and offered concentrated trading via computer terminals. In 1991, six varieties of bonds were traded via the system and the turnover reached 1.637 billion yuan.

The two stock exchanges and the automated quotation system together formed the framework of China's securities market. The establishment of the stock exchanges and the launching of the automated quotation system for stock trading ushered in a new stage in the development of China's securities market and created conditions for establishing a securities market which was open, fair and highly efficient, thus turning it into a standard and unified market.

During this period, reform was also carried out in the securities issue market and some progress was made. One important step of the reform was to adopt the practice of underwriting the sale of certain kinds of state treasury bonds to a consignee group formed by 58 securities companies as well as trust and investment companies. The group bought bonds from the Ministry of Finance and sold them to purchasers. The total value of bonds they contracted to sell amounted to 2.5 billion yuan, accounting for 14.7 percent of the total issue in the year. The financial departments in some places also adopted the method. This reform succeeded in gearing the issue of securities towards the market.

Aside from the issue of new shares, another important step of reform was to issue renminbi special shares, thus opening up a new channel in raising foreign capital. In 1991, the Shanghai Vacuum Electronic Device Co. Ltd. issued renminbi special shares, totalling 100 million yuan in nominal value; the shares were distributed at a premium and the amount of capital obtained reached US$ 70 million. In the same year, the Shenzhen South China Glass Co. Ltd. issued at a premium renminbi special shares totalling 16 million yuan in nominal value, and retrieved HK$ 84.8 million of capital stock.

(4) Accelerated Development (1992): This stage was marked by speeches of Deng Xiaoping during his southern China inspection tour. In the speeches, Deng Xiaoping fully affirmed the experiments of reform to introduce the shareholding system and securities market. This proved to be a powerful spur to the progress of reform. As a result, the securities market reform and economic development helped each other into a new era of development.

In early March 1992, the State Commission in Charge of Economic Restructuring and the State Council Economic and Trade Office jointly held a "Conference to Sum Up Experiences in Experiments of the Shareholding System." Based on information obtained at the conference, the State Council issued a document to affirm the positive impact produced by the experiments in the shareholding system. Later, the State Commission in Charge of Economic Restructuring and other departments concerned jointly issued *Proposals Concerning the Standards of Limited-Liability Companies*, and specific rules and regulations, all of which had played a positive role in institutionalizing and standardizing the trial reform to establish the shareholding system.

The reform of the enterprise system was accelerated, enterprises were pushed into the market, their management mechanism was changed and their organization was restructured in accord with the rules for shareholding limited-liability companies — all this indicated that shareholding companies had entered a stage of standardized development. At the same time, the State Council approved and transmitted throughout the country a report prepared by the State Commission in Charge of Economic Restructuring on expanding the scope of the experiment in the shareholding system and securities market. According to the report, the public issue of shares was extended from Shanghai and Shenzhen to Guangdong, Fujian and Hainan provinces; the number of enterprises which obtained approval to adopt the shareholding system and to publicly issue shares to raise funds exceeded 5,000. These reform steps had laid a solid foundation for expanding the securities issuing market. In 1992, a total of 53 enterprises publicly issued shares in Shanghai; 10 enterprises did the same in Shenzhen.

Under the impetus of reform, both the national debt and the enterprise bond markets quickly expanded. In 1992, the country witnessed the issuing of securities valued at 128 billion yuan (excluding internally issued shares), of which national debts amounted to 41 billion yuan; investment bonds, 2.7 billion yuan; enterprise bonds, 37.9 billion yuan; monetary bonds, 25.5 billion yuan; and shares, 10.9 billion yuan (including 1.2 billion yuan of renminbi special shares). Besides, some new monetary tools appeared. For instance, profit-oriented investment bonds were issued in Shenyang, Dalian, Chongqing and Xiamen; the Shenzhen Bao'an Company issued medium-term stock warrants and exchangeable bonds; the Zibo Township Enterprise Investment

Fund and Shenzhen Tianji Fund were also approved and issued smoothly.

In the state treasury bonds issuing market, the reform of contracted consignment was carried out continuously, and for the first time state treasury bonds were issued without notes. Seventy-three monetary organizations throughout the country formed a consignee group to underwrite the issue of state treasury bonds without notes, with the value totalling 3.645 billion yuan in 1992, and vied with one another for larger proportions of the underwritten amount according to the pre-set deadline for turning in the funds. This not only moved up the date of fund delivery by a wide margin, but also reduced the state's cost for raising funds.

Along with the expansion of the issuing market, the securities circulation market also witnessed vigorous development. In 1992, the total turnover of concentrated trade in securities markets reached 104.41 billion yuan, of which the volume of bonds (mainly state bonds) was 35.127 billion yuan, and that of shares, 69.283 billion yuan. Development was also seen in the trade of shares issued in other places and traded in the two stock exchanges. For instance, five limited-liability companies, namely, the Wuhan Department Store Co. Ltd., the Hainan New Energy Co. Ltd., the Hainan Gang'ao Co. Ltd., the Hainan Chemical Fibre Co. Ltd. and the Zhujiang Industrial Co. Ltd., issued shares on the Shenzhen Stock Exchange; a new addition to the Shanghai Stock Exchange was the Shenyang Jinbei (Gold Cup) Co. Ltd.

Also in 1992, the number of intermediary organizations for stock trade increased, exceeding 1,000 throughout the country — doubling the 1991 figure.

In order to strengthen guidance to the rapidly developing trade in securities, the State Council Securities Committee and the China Securities Supervisory and Administrative Committee were established in October 1992. This represented a step of historical significance in China's efforts to standardize its administration of the securities business.

2. Along with the Continuous Expansion of the Securities Market, the Trading Market System and Securities Market Administrative System Have Been Established.

China's securities market has been shaped by these major developments:

(1) The scale of the securities market has been constantly expanding. From 1981 to 1992, the securities issued amounted to 381.7 billion yuan: 108.4 billion yuan were in state treasury bonds; 39.7 billion yuan in financial bonds; 20 billion yuan in special national debts and value-guaranteed government bonds; 40.7 billion yuan in state investment bonds (including state construction bonds, state key construction projects bonds and capital construction bonds); 96 billion yuan in enterprise bonds; 61 billion yuan in monetary bonds; and 15.9 billion yuan in shares. The total issue of securities in 1992 amounted to 128 billion yuan. On the securities issuing market, the bulk of the lot were government bonds, which accounted for nearly one-third of the total. If added with state investment bonds guaranteed by state finance, they exceeded 40 percent.

The securities circulation market was also very lively in 1992. The total turnover at the concentrated trading market reached 104.4 billion yuan; of that figure, bonds (mainly national debts) totaled 35.1 billion yuan, and shares totaled 69.2 billion yuan, a 13.4-fold increase over the 5.1 billion yuan in 1991. In terms of share transactions, the turnover at the Shenzhen Stock Exchange was 44 billion yuan and that of the Shanghai Stock Exchange 24.8 billion yuan.

(2) In China's securities trading market, a pattern that combines concentrated trade and dispersed trade has taken initial shape. The concentrated trade market consists of two stock exchanges — the Shanghai Stock Exchange and the Shenzhen Stock Exchange; and two networks — the National Securities Trading Automated Quotations System (STAQ) and the National Electronic Trading System (NET). Traded at the two exchanges are mainly private shares issued by the listed companies. After the STAQ system experimented on transactions in state treasury

bonds and corporate shares, the NET system also began to undertake such transactions. The dispersed trade market refers to 3,000 securities trading agencies throughout the country which handle over-the-counter transactions, including securities companies, securities departments of trust and investment companies as well as securities houses established by banks and credit cooperatives.

(3) The securities market administrative system has also been formed. In October 1992, the State Council Securities Committee (referred to as the "Securities Committee" hereafter) and the China Securities Supervisory and Administrative Committee (referred to as the "Securities Supervisory and Administrative Committee" hereafter) were established. The Securities Committee is a state organ that supervises and administers securities markets throughout the country; it is formed by leaders of related ministries and commissions under the State Council. Its basic responsibilities are: doing organizational work for drafting laws and legal statutes concerning the securities market; studying and enacting principles, policies and regulations regarding the securities market; establishing rules and drawing up annual plans for the development of the securities market; giving guidance to, coordinating, supervising over securities-related work in various localities and departments; and providing leadership to the Securities Supervisory and Administrative Committee.

The Securities Supervisory and Administrative Committee is the executive organ of the Securities Committee; it is composed of experts with professional knowledge and practical experience regarding securities. Its main duties are: drafting rules and regulations concerning the management of the securities market; exercising supervision and control over business in securities, particularly shares of securities organizations; enforcing supervision and control over the issue of and trade in securities as well as companies that publicly issue shares; exercising supervision and control over the issue of shares by domestic enterprises overseas; cooperating with departments that collect statistics about securities in studying and analyzing the situation on the securities market to make timely reports and raise suggestions to the Securities Committee.

Some related departments under the State Council and local governments also shoulder some administrative responsibilities for securities: The State Planning Commission is responsible for drafting securities plans and comprehensive balance; the Ministry of Finance is in charge of matters concerning national debts and the administration and registration of accountants and accountant firms; the People's Bank of China is responsible for approving the establishment of securities organizations and their administration; and the local governments are responsible for the management of stock exchanges. The major self-governing organizations of the securities industry are the China Association of Securities Industry and China National Debt Association.

(4) Securities organizations and intermediary organizations have developed quickly. Along with the constant expansion of the securities business, the number of monetary organizations that are allowed to do business in securities and intermediary organizations serving the securities business has also continuously increased. By the end of 1992, of the monetary organizations that are allowed to do business in securities, there were 85 securities companies, 386 trust and investment companies, over 1,200 securities branches jointly established by trust and investment companies and banks, and more than 2,000 securities companies set up by banks and credit cooperatives. The more than 500 securities intermediary and service organizations include mainly accountant firms, auditing firms, law firms, asset assessment firms, credit-rating companies, investment firms and securities investment consulting companies. In order to tighten up control over the intermediary and service organizations and make them improve their services, the China Securities Supervisory and Administrative Committee joined efforts with other departments to work out the qualifications for intermediary organizations involved in securities business. In addition, the membership of the Shanghai Stock Exchange and the Shenzhen Stock Exchange also grew. By the end of 1992, the Shanghai Stock Exchange had 171 members, and the Shenzhen Stock Exchange had 151.

(5) Legislation regarding securities market has been gradually improved. Since the establishment of the Shanghai and Shen-

zhen securities markets, major laws and regulations enacted include *Provisional Regulations Concerning the Management of Securities Trading in Shanghai, Provisional Regulations Concerning the Issue and Trading of Shares in Shenzhen* and *Provisional Rules for the Administration of Securities Companies.* What merits special mention here is socialist China's first *Provisional Regulations Concerning the Issue and Trading of Shares*, promulgated on May 4, 1993. This represented the first step China made towards enacting a universally applicable national law concerning securities markets on the basis of local regulations enacted by Shanghai and Shenzhen; it was also an important economic reform achievement. Proceeding from the realities of China and taking into account international conventions, the regulations were aimed at protecting the interests of the investors, spurring standardization of the securities market (particularly the shares market) and providing a legal basis for operations at the market.

3. The Securities Market Has Played an Active Role in Raising Funds, Deepening Enterprise Reform, Promoting the Development of the Market System, Importing Overseas Funds and Enhancing Citizens' Sense of Responsibility.

For more than a decade, China has experimented with the securities market. This market has developed considerably and played an active role in the country's economic life. It goes without saying that the securities market will go on to produce a profound influence on China's future economic development and economic reform.

The contributions of the securities market are demonstrated by these major aspects:

(1) The securities market has played an important role in raising money, as its role is to turn surplus funds scattered in the society into long-term capital.

When the restructuring of the economic system breaks the highly-concentrated distribution system characterized by unified state control over revenues and expenditures, the distribution of national income will inevitably be more dispersed. But, the scattered funds need to be concentrated again and redistributed so as to meet the requirements of economic development. The channels for such concentration and distribution are monetary organizations, while the securities market is an important monetary channel for concentrating and distributing long-term funds. Through issuing bonds and shares, the securities market turns social funds into long-term funds for economic construction.

Take the government bonds market for example. From 1981 when China began to issue state treasury bonds to the end of 1992, various government bonds issued in China totalled over 200 billion yuan. The funds raised through issuing government bonds have been basically used for economic construction, mainly infrastructure and basic industries. For many years, the state's budgetary allotment for construction remained around 35-38 billion yuan. In 1992 alone, 41 billion yuan of government bonds were issued, exceeding the construction funds covered by state budget. Therefore, the development of a market for national debt has played an extremely important role in raising funds for key construction projects.

The opening of the enterprise bonds market has played an important role in fund-raising for key enterprises, particularly those in basic industries. For instance, in 1990 over 100 large and medium-sized enterprises issued 3 billion yuan worth enterprise bonds. Of the sum, the bonds issued by 24 large and medium-sized power plants reached 690 million yuan; and the bonds issued by 11 major petrochemical works amounted to 730 million yuan. The Shanghai 300,000-ton polyethylene project issued 1 billion yuan in bonds, which proved to be an important guarantee for the smooth completion of its construction. On one occasion, the Wuhan Iron and Steel Company issued bonds totalling 50 million yuan in value, which generated enough money for a technological revamp project.

Though the securities market is relatively small now, it has nevertheless, due to its ability to raise funds, contributed much to the rapid development of enterprises. Since the enterprises which raise money by issuing shares do not need to repay the principal to the investors, they are free of the burden of debt. Moreover, enterprises with sound credit can issue shares at a premium, making it possible for them to raise large amounts of money.

In general, as an important channel for raising funds, the role of the securities market has become more and more evident. For instance, securities in 1992 were valued at 128 billion yuan, accounting for 36.57 percent of the added loans granted that year, which was 350 billion yuan. It is clear that raising capital through the securities market has begun to play an important role in China's economic development. In addition, it can reduce the pressure on the currency policy of the central bank, through which the government raises funds in the securities market for construction, thereby helping stabilize currency.

(2) The development of the securities market will accelerate the pace of market-oriented restructuring of the economic system and promote the formation of a socialist market system.

The importance of the securities market in restructuring China's economic system lies in the fact that it transforms the planned allotment of investment funds into distribution by the market. Under the system of planned economy, investment is the behavior of the government and the funds for investment are allotted by the government according to a plan. On the securities market, however, both the enterprises and individuals become investors; funds are not distributed according to a plan, but by the mechanism of the market: Funds will flow to those enterprises, industries and regions which produce better economic returns and higher profits.

Therefore, the development of the securities market changes the distribution of capital according to plan into distribution by the market, and the market will become the basis for the disposition of resources. That capital enters the market represents an important step of reform China has taken in the establishment of a socialist market system.

Over the past dozen years, China has introduced a series of reform measures aimed at establishing a commodities market.

Yet in terms of a capital market, these reforms are still at a beginning stage. This is because investment is still basically distributed according to government plans; this includes not only the investment funds covered in state budgets, but also long-term loans granted by state banks. This gives rise to a two-way system: on one hand, commodities have entered the market; on the other, capital is distributed according to plan. Under this two-way system, the enterprises have to cast one eye at the market and the other eye at the government. Neither can they shake off their dependence on and interference by the government nor can the market imposes strong constraint over them. For instance, over the past few years, some enterprises produced many products which did not sell well and stockpiles grew bigger and bigger, yet the production went on and the enterprises still operated. The reason behind this situation was that, because of government interference, the state banks supported these enterprises with loans.

It is evident that the existence of protection by the government makes the constraint by the market over the enterprises ineffective. The appearance of the securities market makes it possible for capital to enter the market. With both the commodities market and the capital market in existence, a comprehensive market system comes into being. Within such a market system, enterprises not only shake off their dependence on government interference for development, but also must subject themselves to the objective constraints of the market.

In market competition, enterprises with good returns can have bigger shares of the commodities market and raise funds on the capital market, while those with poor returns will neither have a place in the commodities nor raise funds on the capital market. The mechanism of competition, where the successful survive and the unsuccessful go down, has become both a powerful force and a strong incentive for the enterprises to improve their returns. Moreover, the mechanism of competition can bring about an optimized distribution of resources for it guides capital to flow to those enterprises, industries and regions that generate better economic returns.

Therefore, the securities market not only opens up a new channel for raising funds but also makes the market-oriented restructuring of the economic system develop in depth.

(3) The development of the securities market has blazed a new trail for the enterprise reform.

The goal of the reform introduced for state-owned enterprises is to make them operate independently and be responsible for their own gains and losses. The formation of the socialist market system makes it possible for the enterprises to free themselves from their dependence on the government and gear their operation towards the market. The enterprises can take the initiative to sell their products and purchase the needed means of production, technology and patents on the commodities market; they can also take the initiative to raise short- and long-term funds on the money and capital markets. Moreover, the shareholding system clarifies the propriety relations in the state-owned enterprises: Under this system, the shareholders hold the ultimate ownership, the enterprises operates and shoulders the responsibility for their own gains and losses on the basis of the assets entitled to the legal entities; and the state, like any other shareholders, only shoulders limited liability for shares owned by them. Therefore, an enterprise will be declared bankrupt if it is poorly managed and its assets cannot cover its debts.

Another problem encountered in the enterprise reform is how to make the owners of assets involved in operation of the enterprises so as to enable them to exercise their rights as the owners, while also separate the owners from the managers so as to enable the managers to have full initiative in management. The shareholding system has provided a satisfactory answer to the solution of the problem. In shareholding enterprises, the conference of shareholders and the board of directors ensures that the asset owners are involved in the operation of the enterprises. Under the supervision of the board of directors, the right of management is entrusted to the manager or factory director. This can, on the one hand, ensures that the manager or factory director has a free rein in management, and on the other, avoid some short-term action.

For those shareholding enterprises whose shares are traded on the market, they are also under the strict supervision of the securities market. The reform in the shareholding system and the securities market has proved that all enterprises that have conducted reform in the shareholding system, particularly those that are listed in the securities market, have seen that their managerial mechanism has been greatly strengthened and economic returns improved. Take the five companies first listed in Shenzhen as an example. Their profit increased an average of 97 percent annually, the net value of their assets went up by 2.3-fold, and the amount of working funds raised by themselves made up for more than 50 percent of the total. This forms a sharp contrast with the situation in the past when the profit of state-owned enterprises in the special economic zone went down by large margins, or even heavy losses were incurred for several years in a run.

(4) The development of the securities market has opened up a new channel for importing overseas funds, thus making a positive contribution to opening the country wider to the outside world.

In the past, the import of overseas funds was mainly in the forms of direct investment by overseas businesses and contracting loans abroad. The form of direct investment required that the overseas investors must, apart from funds, have the necessary expertise in the proposed projects, the management know-how and trained people, while the form of contracting loans abroad was limited by China's ability to repay the debts. Compared with these two forms, raising funds abroad by issuing shares is more conducive to absorbing large amounts of idle funds in the hands of individuals and organizations, while the enterprises do not need to take risks in repaying the debts. The securities market provides the necessary conditions for overseas shareholders to increase, transfer and retrieve their investment, and hence holds a great appeal for overseas investment. Due to the development of the shareholding system and the securities market, an increasing trend has appeared in Shenzhen and Shanghai to import overseas investments by means of shares. In 1993 nine major enterprises in China directly issued and traded shares on the international market. Firms and monetary organizations in the United States, Britain, Singapore as well as Hong Kong and Taiwan have one after another expressed their intention to invest in shares in the mainland of China.

The securities market not only has become a new channel to bring in overseas investment but also has created the condition for overseas investors to understand Chinese enterprises and for Chinese enterprises to cater to the international market. The openly quoted shareholding companies must regularly, comprehensively and timely inform the investors, including overseas investors, their state of operation and trend of development; the overseas investors can, on the basis of the information supplied, observe and analyze the developing trend and operation of China's economy as a whole and enhance their confidence in making investment in China. In opening the country to the outside world, the role of the securities market is not limited to simply importing overseas investment.

(5) The development of the securities market has enhanced citizens' sense of responsibility and participation in the economic development of enterprises and the society as a whole.

For the ordinary citizens, to participate in investment through shares means that they must proceed from their personal interests, show conscientious concern for the production and operation of the enterprises and be involved in the process of decision making and management by way of shareholders' conferences, and consequently enabling the enterprises more democratic and scientific in decision making. At the same time, in order to achieve capital gains in the transactions of securities, the investors must show concern for the state's domestic and foreign policies, understand the relevant principles and policies of the Party Central Committee, the State Council as well as the local governments, and, in particular, understand the current operation of the national economy, such as the rates of price hikes, economic growth, balance of international payment, financial taxation and currency supply. All this, in fact, strengthens the supervision by society over the handling of economic affairs by the government, thus propels the government to continuously improve its expertise of policy making in macroeconomic control.

4. The Problems That Call for Earnest Study: the Establishment of Standard Shareholding Enterprises, the Circulation of Publicly-Owned Shares, the Pattern of the Securities Market, the Unified Securities Supervisory and Administrative System, the Improvement of Investor Composition and the Expansion of the Import of Overseas Funds.

In view of the development process of China's securities market, there are now some important problems which call for earnest consideration and solution.

(1) The problem of establishing standard shareholding enterprises.

Transforming enterprises according to the shareholding system must follow certain standards, and the public issue of shares in society and trading in shares must comply with strict principles; this is the foundation for the healthy development of the securities market.

The major manifestations of unstandardness in the transformation of enterprises towards the shareholding system are: First, in their transformation towards the shareholding system, some enterprises did not make assessment of their assets seriously, resulting in the devaluation and losses of state property. Second, when directional raising of funds was undertaken, an excessive quantity of shares were issued to workers and staff within the enterprises, resulting in the abnormal phenomenon of "popularizing internal shares and privatizing corporate shares," which had in turn given rise to black market trading of stock certificates. Third, some places had not transformed their enterprises in line with the demands of the shareholding system according to related state stipulations, rather, they had reduced the standards for enterprises in adopting the shareholding system. Four, in some openly quoted shareholding enterprises, the change of the enterprise management mechanism had lagged behind, the congress of shareholders existed in name only and their rights and interests could not be guaranteed. In view of this situation, the State

Commission in Charge of Economic Restructuring joined efforts with other relevant departments to enact and promulgate some necessary rules and regulations, demanding the local governments and the enterprises do a good job in the enterprises' adoption of the shareholding system according to set requirements. Only those enterprises in which the shareholding system is well established are allowed to issue shares. Blind hankering after amounts of shares issued is prohibited. Assets assessment for enterprises must be earnestly done and the property right must be clearly defined. The enterprises' accounting system must be reformed according to the system required by the shareholding system. Efforts must be made to establish and improve the internal management system of enterprises; the congress of shareholders, board of directors and board of supervisors must be well established, so as to effect a genuine change in the enterprise management mechanism and enhance the enterprises' self-restraining ability. One point that calls for attention here is that, along with the development of opening to the outside world and the enterprises' entry into the international market, the establishment of shareholding companies must gradually comply with international conventions.

(2) The problem of publicly owned shares.

In adopting the shareholding system, China upholds the principle of taking the socialist public ownership as a given mainstay and strives to maintain and increase the value of state property. In terms of the scope of experiment to establish the shareholding system, enterprises that are related to state security and have sophisticated technology for national defense, those involved in the mining of rare metals of strategic importance, and industries and enterprises that are state monopolies will remain state-owned. For energy, transport and communications, telecommunications and other industries that are given priority for development according to state industry policy, the publicly owned shares must constitute a holding proportion in trying out the shareholding system. At the same time, it is stipulated that the shares held by a natural man of an enterprise should not exceed 5 per thousand of the total.

One important question now is that publicly owned shares cannot be traded on the market. One major characteristic of China's reform to establish the shareholding system is the existence of state shares and the high portion the state shares take in the stock right composition. The lack of mobility of a large amount of publicly owned shares neither can give expression to the principle of equality in stock right and ensure to maintain and increase the value of publicly owned shares, nor is it conducive to changing the managerial mechanism in the enterprises. But, the circulation of publicly owned shares involves a series of reforms, such as the reform of the property right system concerning state property, the reform of the state property management system as well as the capacity of the securities market. All these call for earnest study.

(3) The problem of the developmental pattern of the securities market.

In view of the internal structure of the securities market, funds raised through shares account for about 10 percent of the total amount directly raised. For a considerably long period to come, China will stick to the principle of taking bonds as the major part and shares as the auxiliary. But, for some time the market for bonds, particularly for state treasury bonds, was in recession. Departments concerned noticed the problem in a timely manner and adopted effective measures to invigorate the market for national debts.

In terms of the distribution and number of stock exchanges, an obvious gap has appeared between the north and south as well as between the east and west in the development of the securities market. The stock exchanges in Shenzhen and Shanghai have developed very quickly; some other places are also making active preparations to establish stock exchanges. Judging by international experience, in most countries stock exchanges were dispersed at first and later became relatively unified. International experience also shows that unified securities market is advantageous to the reasonable distribution of capital resources, yet it may easily cause monopolies and reduce efficiency. Relative dispersion is conducive to competition and raising efficiency, yet excessive dispersion may easily cause segmentation of the market and unreasonable distribution of resources. Therefore, China must learn from the experience and lessons of other countries in developing its securities market and decide the appropriate degree for relative unification and relative dispersion.

(4) The problem of establishing a unified securities supervisory and administrative system.

In order to ensure that the supervision and administration of the securities market is unified, highly effective and fair, all countries have established specialized securities supervisory and administrative organizations. Some countries, which mainly relied on government departments to administer the securities market in the past, have also, after experiencing one securities market crisis or another, established specialized organizations to strengthen control.

The establishment of the State Council Securities Committee and the China Securities Supervisory and Administrative Committee initially broke the pattern of multi-departmental administration of the securities market in the past and has laid the foundation for strengthening the supervision and administration of the country's securities.

In line with the specific characteristics of the securities market, particularly the stock market, it is necessary to give play to the role of self-disciplinary organizations. Therefore, it is imperative to build the securities associations into genuine self-disciplinary organizations to strengthen self-administration and self-supervision among the organizations that do business in securities. It is particularly important to bring into full play the role of such "economic police" as accounting and law firms so as to strengthen social supervision. It is necessary to bring into full play the role of stock exchanges to strengthen their supervision over the quoted companies, their members as well as the transaction process.

While reinforcing the government's supervision and control over the stock market, it is necessary to make the market mechanism play a greater role so as to establish a securities market supervisory and administrative system, embracing the government department in charge, the self-disciplinary organizations in the securities business and securities intermediary organizations, each of which has its own clearly defined duties and responsibilities and is well coordinated with one another. The initial establishment of a securities supervisory and administrative system so far constitutes an important breakthrough. Yet, there are still quite a number of problems and contradictions, all of which call for gradual solution.

(5) The problem of developing institutional investors and improving the composition of investors.

As the stock market has just come into being, the overwhelming majority of investors in the market are individuals who are not fully aware of the risks of securities investing and who are poorly equipped to shoulder losses. Moreover, they are prone to be influenced by rumors and blindly follow others to take in and sell out shares; this will cause not only losses for themselves but also market fluctuations.

As the stock market continues to expand, it is extremely important to develop institutional investors. As China is currently reforming its social insurance system, various kinds of insurance foundations should be allowed to enter the stock market as long-term investors. At the same time, it is necessary to develop cooperative foundations, which will be managed by specialized people on behalf of medium and small-sized investors. These foundations will reduce the risks normally encountered by individual investors and reap satisfactory returns. Such institutional investors are particularly important in China because they are no longer individual investors but have been changed into legal entities: they will help implement the principle of taking public ownership as primary and accelerate the development of the shareholding system and the stock market. In addition, investment through foundations makes it possible to effectively fight the dishonest activities of those who manipulate the market, restrict gambling speculations, and guide short-term investment activities into long-term ones.

With the establishment of foundations, public shares can be traded on the market and the question of how to allow Party and government functionaries to make investments through shares can be easily solved. The problem now is to speed up the pace of enacting related laws. The development of foundations should also be a gradual course. At present, it is best to only develop open foundations, rather than closed ones. Those who wish to join or exit the foundations should be able to do so at any time, and shares bought with foundation funds should not be transferable.

(6) The problem of using securities market to expand import of overseas funds.

In the 1980s, the main pattern of raising funds in the world shifted from acquiring debts to issuing shares. At the early stage of reform and opening to the outside world, China mainly acquired funds by direct investments from overseas businesses and by foreign commercial loans. The development of the securities market, particularly the stock market, has met the demands of overseas businesses to invest in Chinese enterprises. Hence, importing overseas capital through issuing shares has been put on the agenda.

For foreign investors, both making direct investment and buying shares can accomplish the goal of sharing in China's economic growth. The result is basically the same. However, to make investments through buying shares is more flexible for overseas businesses. The overseas investors choose their fields of investment by selectively purchasing the shares; moreover, investors can respond to China's new policies (and perceived risks) by reducing their investment. These are favorable conditions that direct investments do not possess. Therefore, to absorb overseas investment through issuing shares opens a new and more flexible channel for raising overseas funds.

In 1991, China experimented in issuing B shares, which are sold only to people outside of Chinese territory; this represented the first step in raising overseas funds with stock right. It was basically a success. In 1992, a few Chinese enterprises directly issued shares overseas. Its advantages are: instrumental to enhancing the international reputation of domestic enterprises and making them gear their operation towards the international market; conducive to learning from the advanced management know-how of the securities business in other countries that will help in improving China's management of the securities market.

In 1992, an agreement was reached between the Hong Kong Stock Exchange and the Securities Supervisory Committee for gradually allowing the Shanghai Petrochemical Works, the Qingdao Beer Brewery and some other enterprises to issue H shares in Hong Kong. This represented the opening up of a new channel for the utilization of foreign funds. However, further study is needed on the following questions: How large should the scope be in using shares to absorb foreign funds? What form should be adopted in using shares to absorb foreign funds? And how should China cooperate with related authorities in enforcing supervision and control over the enterprises that issue shares on overseas stock market?

5. It Is Necessary to Further Expand and Improve the Securities Market by Amplifying Necessary Laws and Regulations, Adopting Universal Standards for the Transformation of Enterprises Towards the Shareholding System and Streamlining the Market Operational Mechanism.

In view of the status quo of and problems in China's securities market, securities experts have put forth the following suggestions.

(1) To Make the Securities Market Operate Within a Well-Established Legal Framework.

It is naturally a long process to establish a complete set of laws and regulations concerning securities. Since the establishment of the State Council Securities Committee in 1992, China has made great efforts to enact various laws and regulations concerning securities. The *Provisional Regulations Concerning the Issue and Trading of Shares* was already enacted by the State Council; the *Rules for the Administration of Stock Exchanges (for Trial Implementation)* was promulgated by the State Council Securities Committee; and the *Corporation Law* was put into effect in July 1994.

However, China's legal system regarding securities still leaves much to be desired. In particular, some basic laws, such as the *Law on Securities*, have not been formally decreed. At present, apart from making efforts to establish this law as soon as possible, it is necessary to speed up the pace in drafting a number of related regulations and detailed rules for their implementation, such as *Regulations on Preventing Behind-the-Scene Transactions and Fraudulent Conduct, Regulations on the Management of State Shares, Code of Conduct for People Involved in the Securities Business*, and *Regulations on the Management of Domestic Enterprises Issuing and Trading in Shares Overseas*, so as to help the securities market operate smoothly and develop within a well-established legal framework.

(2) To Straighten Out the Operation Mechanism of the Market.

A well-coordinated market operation mechanism is an important condition for the securities market to play its role fully. In perfecting China's securities market mechanism, it is necessary to both learn from international experience and take into consideration China's situation.

First, it is necessary to increase the transparency of the market, that is, to make market information fully public. In this respect, the work over the past few years dropped behind. The department in charge only demanded to disclose to the public some information when shares were first issued. Investors knew little about the quoted enterprises. The system of fully disclosing to the public information about the quoted enterprises has been clearly written into the *Provisional Regulations Concerning the Issue and Trading of Shares* and the *Detailed Rules for the Implementation of the Stipulation on Disclosing Information About Companies That Publicly Issue Shares*. It should be carried out in earnest.

Second, it is necessary to break down the barriers between regions and promote the formation of a unified market. Over the past few years, much improvement has been made in this respect. Yet, there are still barriers of one kind or another between different regions, and there are still some discriminatory stipulations in the provisions enacted by the local governments concerning the securities market; all this hinders the formation of a national unified market. The solution of this problem should be approached from two angles — improving both the legal system and technology, namely, enacting unified laws and regulations and upgrading the technological conditions of the stock exchanges and their members.

Third, it is necessary to study the question of the circulation of public shares. In the experiment over the past few years, public shares generally were not circulated. On the stock market, only private shares were allowed to be traded, and this made it hard for the stock market to play its role in adjusting the structure of the stock of state-owned property. The solution of this problem is fairly complicated because it touches upon the property right system and administrative system regarding state-owned property.

In addition, it is imperative to bring into active play the role of intermediary organizations in the securities market and to further improve the clearing system and trusteeship of the securities market so as to provide the market operation with a modern technological foundation.

(3) To Standardize the Transformation of Enterprises According to the Requirements of the Shareholding System.

Shareholding companies differ greatly from state-owned enterprises, so does their operation. Shareholding companies have a set of strict rules concerning their internal division of power, distribution of economic returns, system of awards as well as management. For sometime in the past few years, all sorts of enterprises throughout the country competed with one another to introduce the shareholding system without giving full consideration to the state requirements and procedures as well as their specific conditions, giving rise to quite many problems. For some of the enterprises, the change was only superficial: their internal management mechanism and the structure of power in decision making still remained as it was. Some companies withheld import information, causing losses to the shareholders. Therefore, it is necessary to ask the enterprises to adopt the shareholding system and strictly adhere to relevant requirements so as to effect a real change in the enterprise management mechanism and bring genuine prosperity to the stock market.

(4) To Actively and Steadily Expand the Scope of Experiment in the Stock Market.

The development of the market economy calls for actively enlarging the capacity of the stock market to meet the fundraising demands of enterprises. While making efforts to improve the legal system concerning the securities market and the market operation mechanism, China has expanded the scope of experiment in the stock market throughout the country.

In 1993, in line with the state pertinent policies regarding economic growth and the capacity of stock exchanges, one or two enterprises in each province (municipalities) were given approval to publicly issue shares to raise capital. For China, this was an important step forward in developing the country's stock market. It showed that the securities market would provide enterprises greater and greater convenience in raising funds.

For the securities market itself, expanding the scope of the experiment constituted an important test of and backing to the administrative system of the securities market, the operation mechanism of the stock exchanges, service of the securities organizations, as well as the development and improvement of other intermediary organizations. On the one hand, it helps bring to light problems and makes a timely adoption of remedial measures possible; on the other hand, it is conducive to training specialized personnel, thus laying a solid foundation for the market's development.

(5) To Continue Exploration in Using the Stock Market to Attract Overseas Funds.

The trial issue of B shares proves that stock market provides a flexible and effective channel to attract foreign funds. However, in light of problems which cropped up in the issue of B shares, further measures for improvement should be studied to proceed with the experiment in B-shares market.

The issue of H shares on the Hong Kong Stock Exchange has basically been a success. The agreements on law, accounting and joint control between China's mainland and the Hong Kong Stock

Exchange and the Hong Kong Securities Supervisory Committee are a useful reference for raising funds in the securities markets in other parts of the world.

At the same time, it is necessary to further study the major securities markets in the world and get acquainted with their advantages and disadvantages so as to improve China's own practice in raising overseas funds through the securities market.

Section 2 Retrospect and Policies for Future Development of the Shanghai Stock Exchange

1. Review and Summary of the Shanghai Stock Exchange's Five Stages of Development and How to Use This Experience in Establishing Securities Markets in Other Parts of the Country.

The Shanghai Stock Exchange has gradually developed to meet the demands of the state financial department and that of enterprises to raise funds. At the first stage, the market showed a somewhat spontaneous character and certainly constituted a breakthrough. Later, it was gradually understood by more and more people and won support from all walks of life, and so grew into maturity. The Shanghai Stock Exchange has experienced the following five phases in its development.

The first phase, which ran from January 28, 1981, to November 1984, was marked by spontaneous development. At this stage, the market displayed the following characteristics: only state treasury bonds, enterprise internal bonds and non-standard shares were circulated on the market; no standard enterprise bonds and shares were issued. The market was far from being perfect; it lacked necessary legal protection; standard primary and secondary markets were absent and black market trading was in vogue.

In order to balance the government's financial deficit and raise funds for construction, the State Council promulgated on January 28, 1994, *Provisions of the People's Republic of China Concerning State Treasury Bonds*, and since then the Ministry of

Finance began to issue state treasury bonds throughout the country.

State treasury bonds issued at the time did not have specified terms and were allotted by administrative order. Furthermore, they were not allowed to be transferred on the market. All this seriously affected the reputation of the state treasury bonds and brought great difficulties to the issue.

At the same time, people had a rather low living standard at this stage; they lacked understanding of investment in securities and did not have confidence in underwriting and holding state treasury bonds. This not only made it difficult for the issue of state treasury bonds but prepared the ground for off-the-book deals.

Under such conditions, the market for state treasury bonds could not but be one bearing the strong mark of administrative interference. In order to fulfill their allotted quotas, some units resorted to providing their employees with subsidies. The subscribers only needed to pay part of the money to obtain the full bond amounts, and the fund balance was offset by the units. Therefore, so long as the subscribers sold the bonds they held at prices higher than what they paid, they could earn a profit, thus leaving room for black market activities. The black market prices during this period were all below the face value.

As such subsidized underwriting made it possible for subscribers to reap gains on the black market, it in a sense remedied the shortcomings in the issue of state treasury bonds because it spontaneously created a balance in cities where the information industry was well developed and alleviated the difficulties in the issue of state treasury bonds. The secondary market did not appear until September 1986, when the Jing'an Office of the Shanghai Trust and Investment Corporation, which was affiliated to the Shanghai Branch of the Industrial and Commercial Bank of China, officially started doing securities business. State treasury bonds began to enter the standard secondary market by April 21, 1988.

Standard shareholding enterprises had not come into being at this stage, yet experiments were silently conducted in internal fund-raising and internal issue of shares within some 100 enterprises. As internal fund-raising was rapidly introduced in many collectively owned small enterprises, experiments in the standard shareholding system in the city were first carried out in small collective enterprises.

The second phase, from September 1984 to April 1988, was the budding phase. Its major characteristics were: standard shares and enterprise bonds began to appear; the primary market had been improved gradually and the standard secondary market began to emerge; black market trading ran rampant and played a primary role in the secondary market; necessary protection by law was still lacking and administrative orders and regulations remained the major means of guidance for securities business; relatively, a small proportion of people took part in state treasury bond and share transactions, yet the absolute number increased fairly rapidly.

In November 1984, the Shanghai Feile Audio Equipment Co. Ltd. issued the first share ever since 1949, signalling the emergence of the primary stock market in Shanghai. The Yanzhong Industrial Co. and the Aishi Electronics Equipment Co. issued shares in January 1985 and the event proved a success. The issue of shares by the three shareholding enterprises attracted many investors and produced great repercussions both at home and abroad.

In August 1986, the CPC Shanghai municipal committee and the Shanghai municipal government, to strengthen leadership over the experimental work in the shareholding system, delegated power to the municipal commission in charge of economic restructuring to enact necessary policies and see to their implementation. The trial introduction of the shareholding system expanded from spontaneous establishment of shareholding companies mainly on the basis of small collective enterprises to guided and planned introduction of the system in state-owned large and medium-sized enterprises. During this period, the Shanghai Vacuum Electronic Device Co. Ltd., Shanghai Feile Co. Ltd. and the Yuyuan Department Store Co. Ltd. were established one after another.

Along with the development of shareholding enterprises, the secondary market for shares began to appear in Shanghai. On September 26, 1986, the Jing'an Office of the Shanghai Trust and Investment Corporation officially started accepting commissions for over-the-counter business in shares. This marked a restoration of stock exchange business which was suspended in China for over three decades. It became one of the ten most important economic events of the year, arousing extensive attention both at home and abroad. The synchronous development of the primary and secondary securities markets greatly spurred on the experiment in the shareholding system in Shanghai and at the same time prepared the ground for further development of Shanghai's securities market.

Due to debate over the question whether the shareholding system was "capitalist" or "socialist" in nature during this period, the experiment in the shareholding system went through some twists and turns and the securities market developed very slowly. In addition, because people did not have sufficient knowledge about shares, they held back in buying shares that were issued in the early period. When the secondary market appeared, people all rushed to the primary market and even queued up for days to buy original shares. Few people visited the secondary market, however. So, the market and its volume of deals remained small. The prices of shares normally remained at the mark less than 20 percent above face value.

During this period, although fairly standard organizational forms were adopted and the number of shareholders had increased considerably, no fundamental changes unfolded in the patterns of operation of the shareholding companies and the control by government departments in charge, leaving people with the feeling that these companies did not possess anything different from the former state-owned and collective enterprises, except the increase of some shareholders. The performance of these enterprises did not show any marked improvement despite the growth in investment, and the amount of information disclosed to the society remained limited.

The only thing that gave people some gratification was the

annual dividend, which normally remained at around 15 percent of the shares face value, obviously higher than the interest rate for bank savings. Hence, people looked on shares as savings deposits and cared only about the rate of dividends. As a result, the prices of shares were low in the beginning of the year and higher when dividends were distributed; then they basically fell to the level at the beginning of the previous year after the dividends were distributed.

Due to the influence of the external environment, enterprises that had tried out the shareholding system were still managed and operated in the original pattern. They felt even greater pressure in the distribution of post-tax profits because of the additional payment of dividends to the shareholders.

As the variety of shares that could be traded was limited, both the experiment in the shareholding system and the trading of shares could not possibly expand by a wide margin, thus producing a minimal influence on the economic life and among the general public. Yet, the mutual promotion between the primary and secondary markets laid the foundation for further development of the securities market.

During this period, three securities companies came into being. They were the Wanguo (International), Haitong and Shenyin (then the Jing'an Office of the Shanghai Trust and Investment Corporation), which in turn established 11 agencies. Of the total, over 96 percent of the deals in shares and more then 50 percent of the transactions in bonds were made in the Jing'an Office, which was then automatically left with the responsibility to maintain share prices. Although there were not any regulations to limit prices, no sharp rise or slump ever occurred. The securities market continued to develop steadily, healthily and slowly.

Starting in April 21, 1988, state treasury bonds were allowed to be traded over designated counters. This heralded the birth of a standard secondary market for state treasury bonds. However, because no fundamental improvement was made in the conditions for the issue of state treasury bonds, the reputation of state treasury bonds did not improve much. Off-the-book deals at prices below face value still predominated.

Although the number of investors was limited at this phase of development, some of them began to make profit by price gaps on state treasury bonds between Shanghai and other places and make financial investments through underwriting shares. Yet, as the shareholding system experiment was at a standstill, there were few new investors. It seemed that the general public just stood there and waited to see what would happen.

In addition, as economic development became overheated during this period, the government began to tighten control over the growth in money supply and raise interest rates. This reduced the vitality of the economy. Hence, the primary stock market met its first difficult spell. On March 21, 1989, the Shanghai Vacuum Electronic Device Co. Ltd. issued shares for the third round. As few people offered to buy, more than 80 percent of newly issued shares were underwritten by the underwriting group (formed by the Haitong, Shenyin and Wanguo securities companies as well as the Jing'an Office of the Shanghai Trust and Investment Corporation. The stock market and even the securities market as a whole entered a period of depression.

In the third phase, from March 21, 1989 to May 28, 1990, the primary market stagnated and the secondary market was in depression. The features of this stage were: Stock prices nosed down, transactions were reduced and the securities market plunged into a stage of overall depression.

Due to changes in the macroeconomic environment — increases in interest rates, financial stringency and the emergence once again of the debate over the "capitalist" or "socialist" nature of the securities market as well as political upheaval in 1989, large amounts of funds were withdrawn from the securities market. Overall, the securities market was in a sorrowful state: prices of nearly all shares nosed down below their face values.

The fourth phase, from May 28, 1990, to May 21, 1992, was a phase of rapid development. The characteristics of this stage were: the establishment of a stock exchange that fundamentally eliminated off-the-book deals (which had previously ran rampant); the secondary trading market witnessed full-scale development: the variety and amounts of new securities listed increased rapidly, stock price steadily and continuously went up and the ranks of investors expanded swiftly.

At the first stage, transactions in securities were brisk, and at the later stage, transactions in shares became prosperous. At the same time, due to the influence of the old system and craving for quick success, the government interfered too much and the control over stock price was lifted too soon, hence causing the second depression of the stock market.

This phase can further be divided into two periods:

(1) The period of off-the-book deals, which ran from May 28 to December 19, 1990. At this stage, no new shares were issued on the primary market. The secondary trading market was still characterized by over-the-counter transactions. As stock prices soared rapidly, the Shanghai branch of the People's Bank of China imposed price ceilings, resulting in few transactions on the over-the-counter market and rampant off-the-book deals. At the same time, the collaboration between "bulls" and workers at the counters plunged the secondary market into great confusion.

On May 27, 1990, leaders of the Shanghai Municipality and relevant ministries and commissions of the central government attended the International Symposium on the Development of the Shanghai Securities Market. This brought vitality to the stock market which had been in depression for some time. Moreover, many Shenzhen investors went to the Shanghai securities market with large amounts of money to purchase listed shares. As a result, stock prices on the Shanghai market soared up beyond their face values. Since then, the stock market there entered a boom period that lasted for two years. It was not until May 21, 1992, when the Shanghai Stock Exchange lifted all limits over price hikes and falls that the stock price began to drop and the stock market entered a period of adjustment.

As of May 1990, large amounts of money floated from Shenzhen to Shanghai to purchase individual shares of quoted companies. Added with the large quantity of funds arriving in Shanghai from neighboring areas, the total was estimated to exceed 1 billion yuan. Conversely, no new securities were issued and shares that could be traded were valued at only around 65 million yuan. At that time, the stock market in Shanghai had just taken off from its bottom and stock price was very low, so the nominal yield remained at 10 times higher than the face value. The more experienced stock buyers in Shenzhen rushed to Shanghai to invest in the stock market there. As a result, stock prices rose rapidly.

On August 3, 1990, the Shanghai branch of the People's Bank of China announced its decision to limit stock price fluctuations, ruling that price hikes and falls were not allowed to exceed 5 percent; later this was changed to 1 percent. Then, prices on the black market skyrocketed, far exceeding the market's limited quotations. This gave rise to the situation: While the prices on the black market soared, there was little business at the counters and various disputes appeared in off-the-book deals, such as people lending their ID cards to others and unfair collaboration between Shanghai "bulls" and workers at the counters. In view of this, the Shanghai branch of the People's Bank of China, the Shanghai Municipal Administration of Industry and Commerce and the Shanghai Municipal Public Security Bureau jointly issued a document banning the black market, but little was achieved.

As no new shares were issued during this period, the soaring trend of stock prices was difficult to curb; the limits imposed on price hikes and falls made it impossible for the listed quotations to reflect true market prices, rather they gave rise to a rampant black market. Although the black market prices went down in the later stage of this period, its low points were still higher than the listed quotations.

During this period, large numbers of people holding shares were involved in off-the-book deals. Due to this fact there was little floor business and black market deals embodied great risks. The market did not take in many new members. Yet, the general public had always paid attention to the changes on the black market, from which they took a beginning lesson about securities and investment skills. This also prepared the public basis for the opening of the Shanghai Stock Exchange.

(2) The period of growth for the Shanghai Stock Exchange, which ran from December 19, 1990, to May 21, 1992.

From the opening of the Shanghai Stock Exchange to May 21, 1992, when all limits on stock prices were lifted, stock prices underwent an across-the-board rise, with the stock exchange index skyrocketing from 100 to 1,400 points.

Ever since the stock exchange started business, stock prices began an overall rise. On the fifth day, the limit of 5 percent for price hikes and falls had to be changed to 1 percent, and later to 0.5 percent. More than two years after the stock exchange went into operation, the experimental shareholding system remained at a standstill: no new shares were issued.

On the other hand, more and more investors turned to the stock market, their numbers increasing rapidly. Shares that could be traded were far from sufficient in both variety and value, and the gap between demand and supply became increasingly acute. Consequently, stock prices remained high and broke the records of black market prices in almost every case. There was a popular saying at that time, "Buying means earning." So, a peculiar situation appeared: The higher the stock price soared, the more people flocked to the exchange to buy shares.

As concentrated liquidation, clearance, transfer and custody, as well as deals "without notes" had been practiced after the establishment of the stock exchange, off-the-book trading lost its ground for existence, thus fundamentally eliminating the black market for securities, once in vogue and a serious impediment to the normal development of the stock market.

On July 28, 1991, the computer automated transfer system began operation, completely eliminating the drawbacks of manual operation, which were the basis for the survival of the black market.

Trading "without notes" was adopted to utterly oust "black shares" left over from off-the-book transactions. The stock exchange ruled that the problem of off-the-book transactions at the Shanghai Stock Exchange would be completely solved during the period from July 27 to September 16. On September 13, the last trading day before September 16, the volume of business on the stock exchange increased sharply as the "black shares" made the last "triumphant escape." Ever since, the problem of off-the-book deals was fundamentally solved on the Shanghai stock market. The elimination of the black market and the control over stock prices made the shares business volume on the stock market very small. At the same time, however, the bond business volume increased rapidly. Hence, during this period, deals and speculations in bonds were very brisk and the competition for investment in bonds was no less fierce than in shares. A large number of the citizens fervently plunged into investment in various kinds of bonds.

The hikes in stock prices and the continuous reduction in the volume of business made people feel that there were people who wilfully pushed up stock prices. So, in July the stock exchange introduced a "turnover control method," which was amended in September. The method stipulated that stock prices could only be raised to a new level when the volume of business reached a certain percentage. But, it came to little avail. The number of people who were ignorant in investing in shares continued to increase; they completely lacked the sense of risks involved in securities investing.

While devoting attention to strengthening administration and control over the stock market, strenuous efforts were being made to increase the variety of new shares. Since 1991, the Shanghai Stock Exchange had done a great deal of work to increase the variety and amount of shares. Because the state had not approved quotas for new issues, the only feasible way was to increase the issue number of formerly listed shares. This not only changed the situation that companies listed on over-the-counter trading markets were too small in scale, but also increased the number of shares that could be traded on the stock market.

In August, the Feile Audio Equipment Co. Ltd. and the Aishi Electronics Equipment Co. issued 500,000 shares (at 60 yuan per share) to increase their capital by 2.35 million yuan and 2.3 million yuan respectively (calculated according to the face value). The high premiums of the capital-increasing shares further lifted stock prices.

At the end of 1991, the Pudong Volkswagen, Special-Shaped Steel Tubes and Zhongcheng Real Estate shares were issued. As a large crowd rushed to the stock exchange to subscribe the Pudong Volkswagen shares, a few dozen people were wounded (more than ten seriously) and traffic was disrupted. As a result, a decision was made to postpone the issue of the Special-Shaped Steel Tubes and Zhongcheng Real Estate shares (these shares were selected for issue and underwriting in 1992 by a random selection, the first such case in China).

At the beginning of 1991, a new round of trials on the shareholding system was widely talked about. In order to avoid panic purchases of shares, which disrupt traffic and normal social order, the Shanghai municipal government decided to issue the 1992 share underwriting certificates, at a price of 30 yuan each. No limit was set on the number of the certificates that could be bought. The public did not buy very actively the certificates because they heard early in the year that the quotas for the issue of new shares was small.

On March 27, 1992, five new shares were added to the listing: No. 2 Textile Machinery, Jiafeng, Joint Textiles, Light Industrial Machinery and Special-Shaped Steel Tubes. At this juncture, stock prices continued to soar and the public felt the risk of a stock price decline. To keep step with the plan of issuing new shares and foster a proper sense of risk among investors, the stock exchange gradually lifted control over stock prices with the aim to promote the early maturity of the market and the investors. On February 18, the exchange lifted control over the shares issued by Yanzhong Industrial Co. and the Feile Audio Equipment Co. Ltd., and in the ensuing three weeks, the stock prices kept on soaring, from the closing price of 98 yuan on February 17 to the 373.49 yuan closing price on March 12. After that, the prices began to come down, yet it remained at a level still somewhat higher that before the control was lifted. Consequently, some investors who bought in when the price was higher suffered great losses, thus breaking the myth that "to buy in means to profit." But, as no new shares were issued, the 1-percent limit for price hikes and declines on Vacuum Electronic Device and other three varieties of shares, imposed in mid-April, was released to reach 5 percent. Then stock prices began to climb up with fluctuations, reaching the so-called consolidation period. But, the stock prices began to soar again when new shares were issued yet not listed on the exchange. It was not until May 21 when the new shares were released in a concentrated manner and control was lifted completely that the rising trend in stock prices at the Shanghai stock market came to a periodical end and entered a new round of depression.

The major characteristic of this phase is: The interruption in the issue of new shares further sharpened the gap between supply and demand, made stock prices soar and encouraged inexperienced investors to blindly flock to the stock market.

The fifth phase, from May 21, 1992, to the first half of 1993, was a phase of consolidation and depression.

The characteristics of this phase were: Stock prices continuously declined; large numbers of investors left the stock market; the government interfered, but with little result; investors blamed the government; the issue of new shares was locked in the horns of a dilemma; and the volume of business was reduced.

After lifting controls on the prices of Feile and Yanzhong shares, on May 21 the stock exchange lifted price controls on all 15 shares listed and removed limits on price hikes and declines. On the same day, the stock prices skyrocketed, with the Shanghai Stock Exchange Index soaring from 616 to 1265.79 points. It was not until May 25, when the index reached its high of 1420.79 points, that it began to fall. From then on, stock prices kept nosing down, and ended up at 450.23 points on October 30.

Prior to May 21, the ceilings imposed on stock prices, along with the relatively small amount of shares listed on the market, made the disparity between the supply and demand very sharp: a certain degree of control existed over price hikes and declines. The complete lifting of controls on May 21 suddenly released the unspent purchasing power caused by price controls. Stock prices skyrocketed. Then, many people began to dump held shares, because (a) there was a wide gap between the issue price and the market trading price, and the holders of the original shares would earn great profits just by selling out; and (b) the method of underwriting certificates was adopted for the issue of new shares, all of which were concentrated in the hands of a small number of certificate holders; and random numbers were picked to select shares in four rounds a year, causing many people to dump the shares they held for underwriting the next round of new shares. Despite this fact, stock prices dived sharply. The pressure for dumping remained great and nearly all holders of original shares were anxious to sell out their stock.

Because the stock market lacked well-developed facilities, many shareholders found it difficult to sell their shares. People crowded in front of stock dealing agencies all day long trying to dump shares. In order to solve this problem, the stock exchange decided to make stock dealing companies to set up stools at the Shanghai Cultural Square to let shareholders to sell. Under this condition, the selling pressure brought to be borne by the stock exchange had become increasingly heavy and the stock price kept nosing down.

The downward trend in stock prices was beyond anyone's imagination. In a very short time, it had fallen from several dozen times over the nominal value to about ten times above. In order to protect the interests of medium and small investors and make preparations for new issues, the department in charge of securities (the Shanghai Municipal Securities Administrative Committee) demanded that securities dealers buy shares so that the stock price could be maintained more than ten times over the nominal value. As a result, the stock price quietly picked up. On August 10, securities dealers took sudden action to dump shares, causing an unprecedented fall in stock prices. Many investors took the opportunity to buy, causing the stock price to pick up again. During this spell of stock price fluctuations, falling constituted the major trend; nevertheless, the index was maintained at around 700 points. Even the second and third rounds of underwriting failed to cause a rise in stock prices.

In order to save the stock market, the Shanghai municipal government decided to postpone new issues. The announcement, however, did not bring vigor to the stock market. In September, the municipal government decided to adjust the policies regarding the stock market: (a) new issues would be made according to original plan; and (b) corporate units were allowed to engage in deals of individual shares. The measure resulted in only a slight rise in stock prices. To save the stock market and prevent short-term speculation on the part of corporate units, the municipal government in late October again decided corporate units that bought shares were not allowed to sell until seven days after their purchases. With the leak of this news, the stock price nosed down sharply, to a low of 400 points.

From the above, it can be deduced: (a) the listing of a large number of companies produced, in a short period of time, the false phenomenon of share supply exceeding demand, thus causing a fall in stock prices; (b) the method of one-year validity for subscription certificates enabled shares to concentrate in the hands of a small number of people, resulting in a strong selling pressure shortly after listing; and (c) lack of experience and too much administrative intervention on the part of the government caused greater fluctuations in stock price, making share buyers blame the government rather than the market.

2. Lessons Learned from the Shanghai Stock Market.

1) It is necessary to proceed from the inherent law of the market to list companies and quote shares in a steady and continuous manner, ensure a sustained and stable development of the primary market and promote the balanced development between the primary and secondary markets.

The issue of shares must be steady and stable. At the initial stage of development, because of the lack of listing of a number of major enterprises, the Shanghai stock market was small in scale, and the quoted shares were small in number and amount, thus causing a sharp discrepancy between supply and demand.

The stagnation of the primary market seriously affected the normal performance of the secondary market. Between April 1989 and January 1991, not a single joint-stock company issued shares and not single new variety of shares was listed — this made the gap between the supply and demand more acute and the stock prices skyrocketed beyond anyone's expectation. Prior to the opening of the stock exchange, authorities in charge of securities business adopted strict price limiting measures, which instigated massive black market activities. Although the establishment of the stock exchange eliminated black market activities, the small volume of deals it handled seriously distorted the developing trend of stock prices as well as the psyche of the securities investors.

On the contrary, the concentrated listing of a number of shares seriously interrupted the normal performance of the stock market, producing a severe distortion of stock prices and causing a strong artificial pressure on the secondary market. It created the misconception that the supply of shares exceeded the demand in the short-run, thus aggravating price fluctuations and risks. Shanghai experienced this predicament between May and August 1992 and decided to postpone new issues.

The situation of supply falling short of demand is a major feature of a fledgling stock market. Yet, massive issues in a short time may also cause "bearish" sessions on the stock market, hurting its vitality and even producing a harmful impact on social stability at the initial stage of the stock market.

The time for the issue of shares should be decided in accordance with the development of the secondary market. Usually, it is appropriate to launch new issues when the secondary market is "bullish" and the prices are on the rise. If the number of newly issued shares does not result in a crash on the secondary market, that should be considered an appropriate amount. When the secondary market fluctuates or even turns "bearish," it is inappropriate to make new issues.

Securities business experts point out that the issue of shares should be closely combined with their listing. Once issued, the shares immediately face the problem of circulation. Postponed listing after the issue is bound to affect the fluidity and convertibility, both of which are precisely the major characteristics of shares. On the Shanghai stock market, postponed listing of shares after their issue has resulted in new black market trading, particularly black market trading in corporate shares — and there is danger that this practice could spread even further.

New shares should be listed as soon as possible after they are issued, so as to ensure their fluidity. In Hong Kong, new shares are usually listed 20 days after they are issued. Shanghai does not have a time limit now; it is decided at great random, resulting in unequal opportunities for people investing in different kinds of shares to cash and trade their shares and reap yields. This constitutes a violation of the principle of being open, equal and fair.

To protect the rights and interests of the shareholders and carry out the basic principle of being open, equal and fair, experts suggest the following: (a) strictly standardize the requirements for companies that make public bids in the issue of shares, so as to make all companies that issue new shares reach the standards for listing; (b) launch new issues in line with the development of the secondary market and when the market is on a steady rise, the scale of the new issues should be appropriate, so as to avoid causing an excessive crash on the secondary market; and (c) after the new issues are made, they should be listed in a short period of time, so as to protect the rights and interests of the investors. This point should be made clear in relevant rules.

2) It is imperative for the sound development of the stock market to break the yokes of the traditional planned economy and follow the principles of the market economy. These steps should be taken: remove quotas for the issue of shares, decide the scale of the issues in accordance with the situation on the market and allow the stock exchange to mark its own time, so as to gradually overcome the current imbalance in the issue of shares.

The second round of depression on the Shanghai stock market was mainly caused by an excessive amount of new shares and too quick a tempo in the issues, both of which were in turn caused by following the old system. In 1992, the level of new issues in Shanghai was still controlled by the central government. In order to narrow the gap between the supply and demand, which was fairly acute prior to 1992, Shanghai worked hard to make full use of the pre-determined scale, and also applied to the central government to increase the yearly quotas. Instigated by this idea, the relevant departments in Shanghai adopted measures to accelerate the issue of new shares. In 1992, a total of 53 new shares were issued, and the total amount of stock capital, calculated according to the nominal value, reached 11.019 billion yuan, of which 683 million yuan were individual shares.

When the local government took this step, it only paid attention to making full use of the quota the central government approved for it, but overlooked market reactions. This is just like when local governments appeal to the central government for bigger piece of the investment pie. The issue of a large number of new shares made it hard for the market to absorb, thus causing market fluctuations and adversely affecting investors' confidence.

How many new shares should be issued in a year? This calls for careful study. Usually, Western countries issue an appropriate number of new shares at the most opportune moments in line with the specific conditions on the market, whereas our practice is to set a quota at the beginning of the year. If the localities do not use up their quota, it will be reduced the following year. It is very difficult for planned arrangements to conform with the spontaneity of market demands. This situation must be altered.

At present, both the issue and listing of shares are planned. Once the government approves a new issue, it will then ask the stock exchange to make arrangements for its listing or postpone its listing. When the stock price goes up, the shares will be listed; and when the stock declines, the listing will be postponed. As for whether the enterprises issuing shares are up to the standards of the stock market, it is up to the government to decide. In this sense, the government has taken the place of the stock exchange. Although the stock exchange is in the frontline, it hardly has any say over the issue of new shares. So, more often than not, the time for the listing of new shares does not get full consideration, and the stock exchange cannot bring into full play its independent supervisory role over listed companies.

Securities experts propose: (a) abolish the practice of setting quotas at the beginning of the year for new issues; (b) delegate to local governments the power to examine and grant approval to enterprises with regard to setting up or converting to shareholding stock companies (and this process should take into account factors such as what industries or trades the enterprises are in and the quality of their leadership); and (c) make the stock exchange responsible. for approving the listing of the shareholding companies and scheduling the new issues and their listing in line with their plans for the listing of shares as well as their various rules.

This is advantageous to breaking the yoke of plans and quotas; rather, it decides the amount and opportunity of new issues according to market demands. It is also conducive to establishing closer links between the primary and secondary markets and maintaining the market stability.

3) **It is necessary to enact rules for supervision of listed companies, make listed companies sign contracts for listing with the stock exchange, and establish special institutions to be responsible for supervising the behavior of listed companies and accept complaints from the investors, strictly codify the behavior of listed companies and guarantee the rights and interests of investors, particularly medium and small investors, so as to coordinate with the changing of enterprise mechanisms.**

Listed companies fall into the category of public corporations and their behavior is closely related to the interests of the public investors. To codify the behavior of the listed companies is the precondition for guaranteeing the rights and interests of the investors.

At present, many share-issuing companies do not respect the rights and interests of the individual shareholders. Some companies have never called shareholder meetings; some companies have replaced meetings that include all shareholders with meetings of shareholder representatives only; some companies have never disclosed to the shareholders any important economic decisions of the business; some companies have made major alterations of their financial statements and yet refused to reveal the truth to the shareholders even when the alterations have produced a serious impact on the market and caused rumors after their disclosure; some companies have never called board directors meetings — or made the meetings a mere formality — while putting the affairs of their companies under total control of the managers; the major leaders of some companies have speculated on buying and selling of shares; some companies have indulged in illegal buying of their own shares; some companies have resorted to various pretexts to subsidize their workers and staff to buy their own shares while the shareholders knew nothing about it; and some companies have made plans to increase their issue of shares and yet do not seek approval of the shareholders. All this has made it possible for a small number of people close to the managerial body to reap personal gains. Many individual shareholders complained about these malpractices, holding that these companies have cheated the public and government by allowing a certain group of people to control the market for individual shares and use their inside knowledge to rob money from the general public.

4) It is necessary to quicken the tempo of establishing mutual funds, break the bounds between corporate shares and individual shares, raise the rate of returns from investment in shares and immediately set up the mechanism for long-term investments.

It is highly necessary to establish mutual funds, foster the growth of corporate investors that aim at the appreciation of long-term capital and provide guidance to market investment activities. Mutual funds are a collective investment instrument for the public. They pool together funds from common folks, seek gains for them and provide the general public with professional services. Managed by professional investors, mutual funds pay particular attention to investing in shares that are temporarily "under-valued," seeking to increase the value of capital by keeping shares for a long period of time. At the same time, the turnover rate of mutual funds is usually under 50 percent as stipulated by relevant laws and the prospectus for bidding in subscriptions; this also compels them to follow the above-mentioned course.

Due to the massive amounts of money held by them, the behavior of mutual funds is bound to exert a positive influence on the market, thus breaking away from the current phenomenon of a small number of big investors in securities leading the public to make investments blindly. At the same time, it is conducive to changing the practice of dividing shares according to investors and unifying the market, so as to make more organizations take part in stock market activities. Of the total face value of the shares issued in the Shanghai Stock Exchange, the amount of money spent by corporations to buy shares is twice the amount spent by individual share buyers, indicating that corporations spend much more on shares than individual investors. This amount of money, if brought into the market, will no doubt play a dominant role. Therefore, to combine corporate shares with individual shares is advantageous to further increasing the number of corporate investors and better guiding the investment behavior of the public.

Raising the rate of returns from investment in shares is the key to establishing a mechanism for long-term investment.

The current rate of returns from listed shares in Shanghai is rather low, with a year-end dividend standing at 10-15 percent of face value, or below 3 percent if calculated on the basis of issue prices, or 0.15 percent at the lowest if calculated on the basis of market prices. This has compelled investors to pin their hope for profits on short-term speculation, which in turn has plunged the stock market into constant fluctuations, highlighted the negative aspect of the stock market and incited gambling.

This way of investment, which establishes stock prices on the basis of "castles in the air," has deviated from the goal of introducing the shareholding system and the experiment in the stock market, resulted in an unsound psyche on the part of the share buyers and turned the stock market into a gambling house.

Hence, it is necessary to advocate the practice that listed companies, through making profits by themselves, return part of the public reserve funds to the shareholders in the form of donating shares or raising dividends to increase the rate of returns from the investments, so as to foster their sense in making long-term investments. This will also be conducive to making distinctions between listed companies that are successfully managed and those that are poorly managed, providing the investors with opportunities to make rational investment choices and gradually bringing into being a long-term investment mechanism.

All these, coupled with stipulations encouraging long-term investments, will further promote the maturation of the stock market and the investors.

Section 3　Development of the Shenzhen Stock Market and Reflections It Provokes

1. The Shenzhen Stock Market's Four Phases of Development: Start-up, Over-heated Development, Decline and Rise.

Compared with the Shanghai stock market, the Shenzhen stock market started later and yet developed more quickly; the course of its development is more clearly marked. Since May 1987 when the Shenzhen Development Bank took the lead to openly issue shares to the public, the Shenzhen stock market has undergone the following phases of development.

(1) Difficult Start-up (May 1987 to April 1990):

In May 1987 when Shenzhen had accumulated some experience in the shareholding system (after exploration over the previous few years), the Shenzhen Development Bank took the lead to openly issue shares. But, as people were still not familiar with shares and had doubts of the shareholding system, most of them adopted a wait-and-see attitude towards shares. The originally planned issue of 7.93 million yuan was only 4.9 percent subscribed.

In July 1987, Shenzhen established its first state-owned assets management organization with the aim to create conditions for the experimental introduction of the shareholding system. In April 1988, shares issued by the Shenzhen Development Bank were traded; the 1987 dividends distributed were 10 percent of the face value — but even this failed to arouse people's interest.

In March 1989, the dividend was distributed for the second time and its rate reached 35 percent. At the same time, 325,000 dividend shares were given to the shareholders at the ratio of 2:1, and old shareholders were given new stock receipts at the ratio of 1:1. Such a high dividend rate strongly appealed to the Shenzhen citizens, and the demand for shares rose sharply.

In February 1989, when the Jintian Industrial Co. Ltd. openly issued shares, the purchases were very brisk. In the same year, the Jintian Industrial Co. gave out dividend shares at the ratio of 1:1. Consequently, the price of a Jintian share with the nominal value of 10 yuan rose to 20 yuan.

During this period, the variety of shares increased from one to four, the number of securities dealers rose from one to three and the number of people employed in the securities business went up from seven to 30. Nevertheless, the shares still focused on long-term investments, which still rendered the deals rather dull. Of the total amount of shares traded on the market, shares issued by the Shenzhen Development Bank accounted for 2.4-6.1 percent; those issued by Wanke, 0.8-7.3 percent; and those by Jintian, 4.5-7.9 percent.

(2) Over-heated Development (May to November 1990): Instigated by high returns from shares of the Shenzhen Development Bank, starting in May 1990 the Shenzhen stock market gradually became over-heated; people's interest shifted from hankering after dividend incomes to profits reaped from price differentials in buying and selling shares. On the one hand, the issue market plunged into a long spell of stagnation and no new shares were issued, making the supply at the trading market rest for a long time on five varieties of shares. On the other hand, more and more people were lured into the stock market as manifested in the fact that not only funds from some other provinces and municipalities were drawn into the Shenzhen market, but also some overseas funds entered the market via

the overseas investors' relatives and friends in the country.

The sharp gap between supply and demand kept forcing stock prices up. In the months of May and June alone, the volume of concluded deals soared rapidly to 377 million yuan, a 15-fold increase over the volume of all deals concluded in the previous two years. By mid-November, stock prices increased by an average of over 11-fold; the nominal yield went up from 2-6 fold at the beginning of the year to over 71-fold; and the number of shareholders skyrocketed from less than 20,000 to over 100,000.

In order to prevent rapid, sharp stock price hikes and excessive speculation and crack down upon black market transactions, the Shenzhen municipal government adopted a series of measures, including the rise-halt and fall-halt system. This stipulated that both the rise and fall of stock prices in one day must not exceed 10 percent. This was later changed to 5 percent, and then to +1 to -5 percent, which appeared as unsymmetrical limits for stock price rises and falls.

At the same time, the municipal government levied a 0.6 percent stamp duty on buyers; for individual shareholders they imposed a 10 percent regulation tax on the portion of dividend income that exceeded the interest rate of one-year fixed savings deposits; also they instituted a 0.5 percent service charge on the volume of concluded deals of both buyers and sellers. Moreover, it ruled that all deals must be concluded via securities intermediaries.

Although these measures inhibited the excessively rapid rise of stock prices, they nevertheless distorted the market. On one hand, stock prices rose at a daily rate of 1 percent. By November, the total volume of transactions on the Shenzhen stock market ran as high as 6.275 billion yuan, which was 31-fold over the aggregate nominal value. On the other, few deals were concluded within the market and some transactions were made on the black market. The price on the black market was normally 20-38 percent higher than the quoted price. Sometimes, it was even 100 percent higher.

(3) The "Bearish" Market (November 1990 to September

1991):

In mid-November 1990, the Shenzhen municipal government, in view of excessively high stock prices, wild black market transactions and the chaotic order on the stock market, adopted a series of more severe measures for comprehensive consolidation of the stock market, including lowering the upper limit for stock price rises from 1 percent to 0.5 percent; banning Party and government officials from holding shares; levying a 0.6 percent stamp duty on both buyers and sellers; and dealing heavy blows to black market deals.

After these measures were put into effect, Party and government officials as swell as sensitive shareholders took the lead to dump and cash in their shares. In the first few days, there were still people who sought shares — those who had been waiting for several months to buy shares grabbed the opportunity to buy in. As a result, transactions were very brisk. On November 23, the total volume of transactions reached 51.98 billion yuan, a record for the Shenzhen stock market. Later, as word spread that a tax would be levied on price differentials, sales exceeded purchases. The unsymmetrical limits over price rises and falls further accelerated the declining trend in stock prices, which began to decline on November 26, and by mid-December they had plunged.

On July 3, 1991, the Shenzhen Stock Exchange officially started business, and in August all control over stock prices was lifted. By September 6, the Shenzhen Stock Index sunk to around 45 points (the Shenzhen Stock Index took April 3, 1991, as the standard), a decline of 55 points in five months. As a result, the total market value of shares plunged from 7 billion yuan at the highest to 3 billion yuan by the end of September; and the average nominal yield went down from over 70-fold to around 11-fold.

Apart from the role of the market itself (correcting excessively high stock prices in the previous period), stock price declines during this period were also due to measures adopted by the local government. These measures created uncertainty among investors about the government's policies; investors lost confidence, causing panic dumping and sharp stock price declines.

(4) Steady Rising (beginning in September 1991):

After a few months of overall decline and fluctuations, stock prices began to pick up from the September 1991 low. To help the stock market rid itself of the "bearish" atmosphere and protect the interests of investors, the government once again adopted a series of measures. These included reaffirming its policy of supporting the stock market; non-interference in the distribution of dividends; supporting monetary organizations to participate in payment settlements for the market; and appropriately postponing the issue of new shares to reduce stock market crashes. Moreover, as stock prices in the Shanghai stock market rose to a fairly high level, many share buyers turned their attention to Shenzhen. (Since mid-1991, funds flowing into the Shenzhen stock market had been increasing, helping it to pick up.) On November 4, 1991, the Shenzhen Stock Index went over the 100-point mark; investor confidence was restored.

Deng Xiaoping's speeches during his inspection tour of south China in early 1992 made a positive comment on the Shanghai stock market. After mid-February, the listed companies announced one after another their achievements of management and programs for dividend distribution. Shareholders' returns were obviously better compared with the previous year. These factors greatly boosted the enthusiasm and confidence of Shenzhen investors. In March, the Shenzhen Stock Index began to rise steadily, reaching 312 points by May 26, a record high for the Shenzhen Stock Exchange. Later, the stock index came down as shareholders dumped shares to reap profits; new shares would be issued soon; and the Shenzhen city government was conducting investigations into financial organizations and enterprises which speculated on shares with public funds. By June 16, it fell to 233 points. Since then, the market has been in a pattern of steady development with intermittent rises and falls.

In summary, the Shenzhen stock market has taken shape and is continuously expanding. Yet, it is still premature at present, as manifested in violent stock price fluctuations and the absence of well-established self-regulatory organizations.

2. Major Features of the Shenzhen Stock Market: Standardization, Legalization and Internationalization.

After more than a decade's efforts, the Shenzhen stock market has taken initial shape and is on a course of sound and steady development. The major features are:

First, shareholding enterprises have began to turn from being non-standard to standard and legal. A shareholding enterprise community has come into being in the special economic zone, that takes the listed enterprises as the "dragon head," the several hundred enterprises which have adopted the internal limited-liability system as the skeleton and the several thousand limited-liability enterprises as the periphery. Within the enterprises, the organizational structure, management system, finance as well as the open disclosure system have come increasingly close to international conventions and their performance has become increasingly standard. The *Provisional Regulations of Shenzhen Regarding Limited-Liability Companies* and *Provisional Regulations of Shenzhen Regarding Internal Limited-Liability Companies*, both of which were promulgated in early 1992, have provided a legal basis for the performance and management of shareholding companies and made it possible for them to embark on the track of legalization.

Second, the scale of the market has been expanded; deals and investment have become increasingly vigorous. This is demonstrated by these facts: the number of listed companies has increased steadily; the number of securities dealing organizations has grown in large numbers; new varieties of shares, like securities investment funds, have been issued; several fund management companies have been established; incorporated securities organizations have increased in number; the Nanfang (South China) Securities Company and the Jun'an Securities Company have obtained approval for operation; the city's stock exchange and stock registration company began official operation in July 1992; and the number of people employed in the securities trade has grown by a wide margin. Along with increasing concentration in securities deals, computerization has been enhanced and the volume of deals has soared.

Third, after stock price controls were lifted, there have been both ups and downs in stock prices, and the fluctuations have been fairly gentle. The general level of stock prices has a more rational footing because the overall investment environment in the special economic zone has been further improved and the annual profit rate growth of the listed companies has reached 50 or even 100 percent. Stock prices are now linked with the business condition and returns of the listed companies. Shares issued by financial organizations and real estates businesses are favored by investors as are shares issued by enterprises where management policies are steady, internal management is sound, product market is broad and economic returns are desirable. At the same time, the prices of different listed shares went up and down based on their own merits. This forms a sharp contrast with the situation in 1990 when the prices of all shares went up or down simultaneously regardless of their returns. This shows that the investors have matured in making choices.

Fourth, the market operation has turned from dispersed deals and deliveries to concentrated deals and deliveries. The mechanism in which the stock exchange, securities registration companies and securities corporations both cooperate and regulate each other has been formed and the efficiency of transactions has been greatly improved. The scattered and over-the-counter deals of the past have been basically eliminated, and the open, fair and equal image of the market has been established.

While market operation is being gradually improved, the means of operation and the competence of personnel have also improved. The procedures of deals have been computerized and new forms of dealing, such as commissioning by telephone, have been tried out, thus providing the investors with great convenience to enter the market.

Fifth, the stock market has developed from a closed to an open system, and has been gradually internationalized. On November 18, 1991, ten listed companies in Shenzhen successfully signed agreements or letters of intent with Hong Kong or other overseas securities agencies on consignment of renminbi special shares, that is, B shares. The face value of the shares issued was 180 million yuan, and the amount of funds raised through the issue at a premium reached 780· million yuan, about US$100 million. The Shenzhen Stock Exchange and the Shenzhen Stock Registration Company also signed agreements with the Shenzhen Branch of Citibank, N.A., the Shenzhen Branch of Jarding Bank and Associated Press (AP) on the registration, clearing and quotations display regarding the B shares. So far, the performance of the B-shares market has been satisfactory and its operations have been computerized; the response from overseas investors have been favorable, the subscriptions have been active, and the amount of funds for intended purchases of B shares has exceeded the actual issue by more than five-fold.

With regard to listed companies that issued B shares, their internal operation, financial system, open disclosure system and management system have increasingly become internationalized. The direct participation of Hong Kong and famous overseas accountants, lawyers and securities agencies in the issue, and the preparation of financial reports and prospectuses for public bidding on the Shenzhen Stock Exchange's listed companies has greatly improved their management and enhanced their international prestige.

Sixth, market control mainly by administrative means has been shifting to market control mainly by economic and legal means. Important securities laws and regulations such as *Provisional Regulations of Shenzhen Regarding the Management of the Issue and Transaction of Shares, Provisional Regulations of Shenzhen Regarding the Management of Renminbi Special Shares, Provisional Regulations of Shenzhen Regarding the Management of Securities Organizations, Rules Regarding Business in the Shenzhen Stock Exchange*, and *Rules Regarding the Issue and Clearing Business of B Shares in the Shenzhen Stock Exchange*, have been promulgated and put into effect in a succession. All these have provided a legal basis for deals in and management of securities.

While making efforts to improve securities legislation, new economic methods have been tested to regulate the stock market. For instance, issuing stocks at a premium, institutional investment regulation, the regulation fund and the tax lever have been successfully tried out. With regard to stock prices, the government and departments in charge no longer intervene.

Seventh, the composition of shareholders has been readjusted, the sense of risks has been enhanced on the part of the stock buyers and their market behavior has tended to be more steady and mature. Of the total amount of shares circulated on the secondary market, the proportion held by individual shareholders was as high as over 90 percent prior to the first half of 1991; it has come down to around 60 percent. With necessary control and approval, some monetary institutions and enterprises are now allowed to invest part of their own funds in shares; they are relatively stable in their investment behavior and display a long-term outlook. This, to a certain degree, has been a stabilizing force in the market. Even on the part of the individual investors, their sense of investment risks has also been greatly enhanced, and their investment and operation skills have improved after experiencing the 1990-91 violent stock market fluctuations. In the past, they mainly followed the lead of the big stock speculators and were easily manipulated by these people and rumors. Now, many investors base their decisions on technical analysis of the stock market. As a result, short-term speculation has declined and long-term investment has increased. This has been a key factor in nurturing the sustained and stable development of the stock market in recent years.

Eighth, the ranks of people employed in the securities business have expanded and their competence has improved. They have moved from manual to computer operation, their sense of law and quality service have been enhanced, and the incidence of malpractice for selfish ends and insider trading has been greatly reduced. The plan for long-term development of the stock market has become clearer.

3. Conclusion Drawn on Situation in Shenzhen Stock Exchange: China's Stock Market Has Its Own Features and Faces Many Difficulties for Further Development.

Judging by the situation in Shenzhen, all the listed companies and shares are organized and issued in line with international conventions. Compared with other countries, however, China's stock market has its own obvious characteristics and its development faces great difficulties. They can be summarized as follows:

First, stock markets in developed countries have been in operation for several dozen years or even several hundred years. For them, a complete range of highly efficient and standard operational forms and legal systems have formed; most of them have entered the stage of consolidation and maturity. China's stock market, which started only a few years ago with the experiment in Shenzhen, it is still in an initial stage. It is still far from being mature and lacks experience in both practical operation and market management. So, some difficulties and problems are inevitable.

Second, stock markets in developed countries are built on the basis of a shareholding economy. Shareholding enterprises are the mainstay of the capitalist economy and their standard operation creates a sound precondition for the development of a stock market. In China, however, the economic structure has been mainly built on enterprises owned by the state; shareholding enterprises have been formed on the basis of these state-owned enterprises. During the course of the reform, many difficulties must be overcome in the evaluation of assets, stock reorganization, reform of the internal management and accounting systems, and the establishment of an open information disclosure system. At the same time, it is bound to suffer from the restriction of old concepts and old systems, so China's shareholding enterprises can only be established one-by-one, as the conditions ripen. This cannot but produce an adverse influence on the scale of the stock market.

Third, stock markets in capitalist countries are established on the basis of a market economy. Market activities over the years have trained large numbers of market operators, investors and managers who are well versed in investment affairs and management and have a good sense of investment risks. The Shenzhen stock market, however, came into being at a time when the market mechanism was still developing, the general rules of market operation had not yet been accepted by the public. Malpractice and unhealthy tendencies prevailed. Shareholders at this time had not developed a true sense of investment risks and investments were made blindly. Also, the expertise of the market operators was not high; and market regulations fell short of the demands of market operation.

Fourth, stock markets in capitalist countries are built on the basis of a private economy. Speculation in shares and the behavior of listed companies have nothing to do with the government. The government does not take responsibility for losses incurred in stock market investment, the closing and bankruptcy of companies or in suicide by "jumping down from a high building." China's economy is mainly based on the publicly owned sector, and it is imperative to uphold this socialist orientation either in shareholding system reforms or in the development of the stock market. The government must make strenuous efforts to maintain the stability of the stock market and protect the interests of the majority of shareholders; it must not advocate a policy that allows some people to get extremely rich through speculation while others are plunged into poverty. And it is the government's responsibility to ensure that people do not jump down from high buildings to commit suicide because their enterprises have gone bankrupt or the market has collapsed.

Fifth, most stock markets in other countries are national or even international, and are part of a network where domestic funds can flow freely throughout the country (or even throughout the world), information can be freely exchanged, deals can be easily concluded and investment choices can be freely made. China still lags far behind in this respect.

These differences will exist for a long time to come, because China must, in introducing the shareholding economy and experimenting in the stock market, pay particular attention to combining its specific conditions with international conventions and combining policy objectives with market laws.

By learning from international experience, the Shenzhen stock market has given expression to some unique Chinese characteristics, which can be summarized as follows:

(1) In listed companies whose stock right is relatively more scattered, publicly owned equity has taken an obviously advantageous position. In all listed companies, the publicly owned equity (including the equity owned directly by the state and the equity owned by state units and collectives among other corporate equities) accounts for about 50 percent; individual equity accounts for 37 percent; and equity taken by foreign investors, 13 percent. In the first group of six listed companies, publicly owned equity accounts for about 45 percent, of which the equity owned by the state accounts for 20 percent. In the ten companies which were listed with approval at the end of 1991, publicly owned equity made up 54 percent, which is composed of state-owned equity alone. From this picture, it can be seen that publicly owned equity occupies an absolute holding position; although the proportion of individual equity is also as high as 37 percent, it is nevertheless scattered among thousands upon thousands of shareholders and it can in no way form a threat to the leading position of publicly owned equity. Moreover, along with the shareholding system reform and the listing of shares, the rate of appreciation of state-owned assets has also been greatly accelerated. State incomes from taxes and profits, and income from the issue of shares at a premium as well as stock price differentials have also increased year by year.

(2) As of 1991, the issue of both renminbi common shares and renminbi special shares have all been incorporated into the state plan, while it has been left to the Shenzhen city government and related departments to choose the specific enterprises and industries that are to issue shares according to the industrial policy of the special economic zone. Control has also been strengthened over listed companies, securities dealing agencies and the behavior of the investors through various economic, legal and administrative means; and illegal issue and dealing have been

basically brought under control. The stock market has become more stable and it has gradually entered a controllable orbit.

(3) In order to prevent the gap in returns from being excessively wide and ensure the dominant position of publicly owned equity, in the relevant laws and regulations of Shenzhen as well as the constitutions of the listed companies, it has been clearly stipulated that the nominal value of shares held by a single individual shareholder must not exceed 50,000 yuan; and the shares of a given company he or she holds must not exceed 0.5-1 percent of the total shares of the company. The government has enacted laws and regulations to protect reasonable and lawful investment and speculation, crack down upon illegal investment and hold in check excessive speculation. At the same time, it has levied stamp duties and income tax on dividend incomes.

(4) The *Provisional Regulations of Shenzhen Regarding the Management of the Issue and Transaction of Shares* stipulates: Party and government employees, armymen in active service, people employed in the securities trade and workers in departments related to securities are not allowed to buy and sell shares. To prevent insider trading, Shenzhen also decided that at the current stage securities agencies must not conduct their own business in securities. In both the processes of issue and transaction, attention has also been paid to implementing the "open, fair and equal" principle, cracking down on illegal transactions and abusing one's power for selfish ends, and seeking supervision from the general public. Serious punishments have been meted out to violators of the law and related rules.

Chapter 2
The Issue Market

Section 1 Problems Encountered by China's Issue Market

The stock issue market is the primary way for securities to enter the market. The task of the issue market is completed when the issuers (industrial and commercial enterprises as well as the financial departments of the government) sell securities to the original investors through securities houses and other intermediary organizations. One very important component of the stock issue market is the issue of shares, which involves many walks of life and has a strong nature of speculation. Any mishandling in the issuing process can produce disastrous results.

In China, "stock crazes" sweep over the land when the people's monetary sense is awakened up to the appeal of shares. In the center of the wave is people's hunt for original issue shares.

Original issue shares refer mainly to shares quoted in stock exchanges that are issued at nominal value prices or at prices a little bit higher than the nominal value. As there is usually a large gap between the prices of such shares and the prices of shares that are traded on the secondary market, the possession of original issue shares creates the possibility to gain returns which are several or even several dozens times higher than the original investment.

1. The Issue Prices Are Irrational.

At a mature stock market, the issue prices of shares are usually decided through competitive bidding between the underwriting companies, and they are more rational in that they can reflect not only the natural value of the shares but also the relations between the supply and demand on the stock market. Nevertheless, the issue prices on China's stock market are often calculated by either the underwriting companies or the issuing companies alone. Moreover, the ways of calculation are often varied and subject to human wishes. Some are made by reference to the profit rates on the market, others take into consideration the factor of open reserves, and still others take into consideration credit standing. Consequently, the issue prices are multifarious and extremely irregular. In 1992, the nominal value of each share in the Shanghai Stock Exchange was 10 yuan, its issue price averaged 45.12 yuan, with the highest reaching 92.8 yuan. As a result, the premium level was far divorced from reality, the initial profit far outstripped actual profit, hence greatly jacking up the psychological value of every share and resulting in a situation where the trading price on the stock market remained high for a long time.

2. The Time of Issue Is Irrational.

At present, the stock issue market is heavily subject to administrative interference. It is particularly so in terms of the issuing scale and time, which are exclusively decided by relevant administrative departments beforehand and often fall out of step with the cycle of fluctuations on the stock market. When a "bullish" session comes, the list and amount of shares cannot be increased automatically. And when the session is "bearish," shares are still issued in the pre-decided amount and scope. The companies can in no way choose the best time to issue shares at the best prices, neither can they make use of the level of issuing shares in adjusting the supply and demand.

3. The Forms of Issue Are Not Standardized.

Now, the shareholding system is in a trial stage in China, and the situation whereby the supply of original issue shares falls short of demand cannot be fundamentally changed in a short time. In order to implement the principle of "being open, equal and fair" in the issue of shares, many places in China adopted the method of drawing lots to decide the underwriters. Even this method has some unreasonable aspects. For instance, there are large gaps between the issue and trading prices. When someone gets the lots for the allotment, he will be entitled to lucrative premium returns. Later, some places and companies introduced the so-called "institutional corporate shares," which were said to be shares between the corporate shares and personal shares. In fact, they were "relation shares" and "power shares" resulting from "privatization of corporate shares." The consequence is dreadful to contemplate.

4. An Obvious Pang Existing in the Operation Mechanism of the Issue Market and the Trading Market.

An obvious mark of administrative interference was observed in the choice of enterprises trying out the shareholding system, the number of shares to be issued, the time of the issue, as well as the issue prices of shares, as they must be subject to administrative approval. On the trading market, however, trading activities gradually expanded and the price level on the stock market was adjusted through bidding. The difference in the operation mechanism resulted in wide gaps between the issue prices and trading prices. For instance, in Shanghai the average profit rate for quoted shares was 184 times the issue prices while the profit rate on the market for new issue shares was around 20 times. The potential returns from the issue prices of shares inevitably simulate the craze in purchasing new issue shares.

5. Contradiction Between the Issue of Shares and the Adoption of Shareholding System by Enterprises.

Standard shareholding enterprises are the basis for the issue of shares. China's relatively small-scale share issuing in recent years results from the sluggish pace at which enterprises are adopting the shareholding system. Apart from slowness due to ideological confusion, this situation is also closely related to the current enterprise management system. Proceeding from their own interests, many enterprise managers oppose the shareholding system, which imposes strict conditions in terms of property rights. Departments in charge of large enterprises also worry that the adoption of the shareholding system would put an end to their authority over the enterprises and others would get the windfalls. So they are also reluctant to adopt the system. Moreover, the binding force imposed on enterprises by credits from bank is not strong: not only are the cost of bank loans low, also enterprises can always find excuses to refuse returning the loans. Under such a situation, enterprises lack interest in raising funds through direct channels.

6. Hidden Danger of Credit Inflation Due to the Expansion of the Stock Market.

Now, most local enterprises in China raise funds by issuing shares for capital construction. There is the danger that the expansion of investment scale might cause credit inflation. Enterprises' "hunger for investment" cannot be quenched when most shareholding enterprises only pay attention to the superficial transformation of the property right relations and have not conducted fundamental reform of the property right system and management mechanism. The cause for this lies deep in the current system of economic operation.

7. Contradiction Between the Development of the Stock Market and the Development of the Money Market.

Generally speaking, the amount of money needed by the stock market and the funds available in the money market must be in sync. But the possibility of massive gains from securities makes the demand for funds by the stock market extremely unstable. The interest rates for bank deposits are administrative interest rates restrictive in nature; they lack the sensibility and flexibility to show the changes in the demand for money, and therefore it is impossible to adjust the comparative gains of bank savings and securities purchases with the interest level in order to balance the money supply and demand on the stock market.

8. Discrepancy Between the Development of Issue Market and the Development of Trading Market.

Now, open stock trading is only allowed in the Shanghai Stock Exchange and the Shenzhen Stock Exchange. Yet, many places have issued shares but cannot trade them. This has given rise to wilful black market trading. From time to time, swindles take place which lead to disputes over equities. At the same time, obvious discrepancies exist in the operation mechanisms of the issue and the trading markets. The stock issue market bears a heavy tint of administrative interference, while the activities in the trading market have gradually opened: the share prices are adjusted through offers and counter-offers between the sellers and purchasers. This results in excessively large gaps between issue prices and trading prices, which inevitably goad on the purchasing craze for new issue shares.

In addition, there are many irregularities in the management of issues and underwriting of shares. Also, there is the problem of state interference in the stock market. To tackle these problems, many scholars have proposed numerous solutions — some lay stress on improving techniques and others call for strengthening control over the issue and underwriting of shares. Nevertheless, they all agree on the need to select a new model for the issue of shares. Therefore, it has become an extremely urgent task to study and decide upon a new stock issue model which is suited to China's national conditions.

Section 2 Comparison of Stock Issue Models

1. Model One: Issuing Great Amounts of Stock Underwriting Forms for Drawing Lots to Decide the Underwriters.

Before shareholding companies openly issue shares, their underwriting organizations can issue stock underwriting forms to the public. In making the forms, attention should be paid to the following points: (a) the forms should only be valid for the current round of stock issue; (b) the number of forms distributed shall be limited; (c) the forms must be sequentially numbered for drawing the lots; (d) the price of each form should not be over 2 yuan; and (e) the forms should be printed with the note "Read carefully the tender invitation prospectus before filling the form." In addition, the forms should also be printed with the name of the shares to be issued, the amount allowed to be underwritten as well as the allotment method. The underwriting forms should be issued on the day when the prospectus is make public and the duration of the issue should not be too short, normally 10-15 days. Prior to the issue, the underwriting organizations must disclose to the public in newspapers designated by China Securities Administrative and Supervisory Committee, the starting and ending dates of the issue and the addresses where they can be obtained. During the issue, each form must be attached with a photo of the person intending to buy the shares. When the issue is ended, the major underwriting organization must verify, sort out and analyze the forms, and then decide the winners by drawing lots publicly under the supervision of representatives from a public notary organization. Those who win the lots can take a copy of the form and his or her ID card and go to places designated by the underwriting organizations to turn in the money in ways determined by the underwriting organizations.

This model was adopted fairly early in Shenzhen and had been continuously improved. Its advantages are: The issue is relatively scattered, and as such the role of securities houses in other places can be brought into full play in sharing the burden; it can be easily carried out; and it accords with the psychology of the public. Its shortcomings include: It has not taken into account the funds people have for investment — those who have the money might not be able to buy the shares and those who do not have the money might be the winners of the lots. Consequently, it inevitably gives rise to a black market for the winning certificates. At the same time, it fails to fill the gap between the primary stock market and secondary market.

2. Model Two: Issuing and Underwriting Shares Through Invitation for and Offering of Bids.

The whole process is divided into two stages. First, bids are invited and applied between the share issuing companies and stock underwriting houses for the consignment of shares. Second, bids are invited and applied between share underwriting companies and investors. The specific steps of the first stage are: When the application submitted by a share issuing company to raise funds through issuing shares is formally approved by relevant departments in charge, the issuing company can then start inviting bids from securities houses. The bid offers should include: the price for the underwritten issue of the new shares; the duration of the issue underwritten; the underwritten amount; and the advantages of the underwriting houses. Those securities houses that intend to underwrite the issue can prepare and turn in their bids which should include the above-mentioned contents within the specified period of time; having received a large amount of bids, the share issuing company compares the bids and decides the winning securities agency or agencies; the issuing company and the winning agency sign an underwriting agreement; and the issuing company announces in newspapers a prospectus for bids and the name of the winning underwriting agency.

At the second stage, bids are invited by the winning underwriting agency and given by the investors. The specific steps are: The winning underwriting agency announces in relevant newspapers a prospectus which includes the price and amount underwritten as well as the time and place to enter bids; the investors go to the designated place to complete the underwriting formalities with the winning underwriting agency, and pay the warrant money according to the price offered and the amount of shares they subscribed; the underwriting agency makes a list of the prices offered by the investors, selects a certain price range as the winning range, decides the selling price of shares according to the price range and makes public the winning price range and the selling price; the investors who have won the bids go to the securities underwriting agency on the pre-decided date to complete the delivery formalities; and at the same time the underwriting agency returns the warrant money to those investors who have not won bids.

The advantages of this model are: It is able to mitigate the phenomenon of panic purchasing of shares issued; it is conducive to associating the primary stock market with the secondary market so that all investors can be equal in terms of the risks and opportunities. The disadvantages are: the possibility of causing the premium to be too high, and so making the shares lose appeal to the investors.

3. Model Three: Issuing Lots That Can Convert into Stock Option Certificates.

After making public its advertisement for underwriting, the shareholding company which issues shares first decides the issue price of the shares and then makes full use of the monetary network to publicly distribute lots, in the form of drawing cards — the amount to be distributed should not be limited. (This happens within a specified period of time.) In order to facilitate card trading, they are issued without the names of the purchasers written on them. The cards should be sequentially numbered. So it is easy to collect statistics, the cards can be picked level by level downward. The price of each card should not be higher than 10 yuan. When the issue of the cards is completed, one lot drawing should be held to select all the winning numbers. Winning cards automatically and unconditionally convert into stock option certificates; they can be traded immediately on the market. The places where they are traded are the Shanghai Stock Exchange and the Shenzhen Stock Exchange, and the trading duration is one to three months. When the trade in the underwriting cards ends, holders of the underwriting cards must pay for their shares.

The advantages of this model are: It connects the primary stock market and secondary market, so that there will not be a gap between them; it can avoid black market trading in the lot-drawing cards; and as the lot-drawing cards are not necessarily issued in printed form, it saves costs and greatly simplifies the procedures.

Its disadvantages are: As the stock option certificates can be traded on the market, it blurs the distinction between the issue market and the secondary market. In addition, as the duration of the issue is comparatively long and the scope of the issue is limited, the certificates have to be traded over the counter in places where there are no members of the Shanghai Stock Exchange and the Shenzhen Stock Exchange.

4. Model Four: Paying Warrant Money in Advance.

When a share issuing company places its public advertisement for underwriting, it has already decided the total amount of shares to be issued, the issue price, as well as the minimum amount of warrant money to be paid. Investors go to the designated securities underwriter to turn in their warrant money for the shares; the amount of the warrant money is not limited. When the specified time for delivering the warrant money is ended, the securities underwriter and the share issuing company decide and announce the price of the shares to be issued in line with the total underwriting and the total amount of warrant money turned in. When the investors see the announcement, they go to the securities underwriter to complete the stock delivery procedures.

The advantages of this model are: It is uncomplicated and practical, and has taken into account the factor of purchasing power. The disadvantages are: It may cause the premium to be too high and hence cause investors to lose enthusiasm for investment, thus defeating the purpose of the issue — raising money.

5. Model Five: Using Fixed Amount Deposit Stock Option Certificates.

First, a share issuing company decides an underwriting group for the shares to be issued through a bid invitation and then publishes a notice for underwriting in newspapers designated by the Securities Supervisory and Administrative Committee. The underwriting group has one major executive and several deputy major executives; the major executive is responsible for the distribution of the fixed amount deposit certificates throughout the country. The specialized banks and securities houses in various places then distribute the certificates to all selling networks. The fixed amount deposit certificates are made by the underwriting group. The amount fixed for each such certificate is determined according to the ratio between the nominal value and the premium. The issue price of the shares is decided according to the net worth and post-taxation profit as well as conventional international principles: It cannot be too low, for too low an issue price would reduce the amount of funds to be raised and, moreoer, it may cause too large a price gap between the primary stock market and the secondary market; it cannot be too high, either, for too high an issue price may hurt the enthusiasm of the investors, delay the selling of the shares and incur losses for the underwriters.

Universally numbered throughout the country, the certificates cannot be circulated and mortgaged, and the owners themselves shall be responsible if they are lost. The buyers need to fill fixed amount deposit stock option certificates, and the amount of the certificates they want to buy is not limited. When the distribution work ends, the rate of the winning numbers, that is, the rate between the amount of the shares issued and the amount of the deposit certificates, is first decided. Then, the lots are drawn for the winning numbers on a specified date under the supervision of a notary organization. On the same day, the sub-underwriters are informed the winning numbers, and winning numbers should also be announced in newspapers. In turn, the sub-underwriters inform the various banks of the numbers and the banks automatically convert the deposit certificates into shares. Winners take their deposit certificates and ID cards to go to the banks where they deposit their money to obtain shares. Certificates that do not have the winning numbers are then turned into fixed or open savings deposits.

The advantages of this model are: It is economical and safe, and guarantees that funds are raised in a timely way. In addition, it gives full expression to the "open, fair and equal" principle for investment through shares, and actualizes the principle that "Everyone is equal before law" into "Everyone is equal before ability of investment." In this way, it makes it possible to completely do away with the various malpractices that might arise by issuing lot-drawing forms. Moreover, it can overcome the egalitarian practice of equal allotment or proportional allotment. At the same time, it can effectively attract the funds of the rich and thus serves as a channel for the rich to make industrial investment. Simple and easy in practice, this can be considered a highly satisfactory model in the issue of shares.

Section 3 Determining the Price of Openly Issued Shares

1. Scientifically Determining Share Prices Is Vital to the Successful Adoption of the Shareholding System.

The issue price of shares is a vital factor closely related to the efforts of enterprises in raising funds as well as the success or failure of the reform aimed at establishing the shareholding system. If an enterprise sets an excessively high issue price for its shares, the investors will be reluctant to buy because of the minimal returns and high risks embodied. Consequently, the enterprise will not be able to raise needed funds and achieve a rational adjustment of its capital and stock mix. Ultimately, the business will fail in its efforts to adopt the shareholding system.

Conversely, if the issue price is too low, the enterprise will gain relatively less premium incomes and the cost of funds will increase. Moreover, excessively low issue prices will not be conducive to maintaining and increasing the value of the enterprise's original assets. Therefore, it is of primary importance to determine the price of shares rationally.

As more and more state-owned enterprises are turned into shareholding enterprises and their shares are traded on the Shanghai and Shenzhen stock exchanges, the question of how to determine issue prices of shares calls for urgent solution.

Some events already occurred help show the importance to solve the problem in the development of China's stock market. On June 21, 1992, when four companies in Xiamen issued stock underwriting forms, 600,000-700,000 people queued up all the night for panic purchasing. On August 10, 1992, when underwriting forms for shares to be issued by seven companies were distributed in Shenzhen, over one million people queued up for dozens of hours in rain. When they got word that many of the forms were being held back, they went on strike. Some people went to the countryside to buy other people's ID cards (because

ID cards were needed to buy the forms) and hired rural laborers to stand in the queue to buy forms on their behalf. Some security business insiders, abusing their power, withheld large numbers of underwriting forms and then either sold them at higher prices or waited until the lottery was held and sold the winning forms at astounding prices; still others bought shares first and then sold them at a huge profits.

It is evident that, while promoting reform, the issue of shares also causes, to a certain degree, corruption and unfair deals. At any rate, it is instrumental to enacting and adopting correct policies for the sound development of the stock market to study the reasons lying behind these facts.

In the market economy, the prices and amounts of commodities are determined by the supply and demand on the market. Similarly, the market prices of newly issued shares are also decided by the supply and demand on the market. In view of the situation on the stock market, this helps explain the phenomena of corruption and unfair deals taking place there.

At present, issue prices of shares fall into the following categories: (a) Issue at nominal value: The shareholding enterprises sell the shares they issue at the face value of the shares. This method is mainly suitable for newly established shareholding companies and the pattern of underwriting by shareholders. Its advantage is that it assists in dividing the rights and interests of the shareholders. (b) Issue at current price: This means that the issuing company takes the share price on a particular date or the average share price in the past month on the secondary market as the basis and issue its shares at a lower price than it. This is mainly suitable for deciding the price of shares newly issued by already listed enterprises. This makes it possible for enterprises to raise more funds with relatively fewer shares. (c) Issue at mid-point price: This means to fix the price of new shares according to the median between the nominal value of the shares and the price on the trading market. This method is appropriate for enterprises that issue shares for the first time as it can reduce both the risks in raising funds and the costs of funds. (d) Issue at discount price: This means to issue shares at prices lower than the nominal value. This method is only used when enterprises meet difficulties in raising funds.

2. Issue Prices of Shares Are Too Low and the Price Differential Is Narrow; Primary Market Prices Are Detached from Secondary Market Prices; and the Methods Adopted in Share Issuing Are Improper.

Most of China's shareholding enterprises are established on the basis of former state-owned enterprises. The issue prices of their shares should formulated by taking reference to not only the issue prices of shares of newly established enterprises but also the prices of new shares issued by enterprises whose shares have been previously quoted on the market; they should be decided according to the median point of the two. At present, the issue prices of shares issued by enterprises openly listed in the Shenzhen Stock Exchange are formulated by referring to two factors: the reference price and the regulatory price. The regulatory price can be overlooked. The reference price is calculated according to the following formula:

$$\text{Reference price} = M \times (A \times 0.25 + B \times 0.5 + C \times 0.25)$$

In the formula, "M" = market price of each share now/ dividend of each share, universally multiplied by 15;

"A" refers to the profit of each share in the year before the issue of the shares (after tax);

"B" refers to dividend of each share in the year when the shares were issued (after tax);

"C" refers to expected dividend of each share in the year after the shares were issued (after tax).

The formula contains some unreasonable factors:

(1) The nominal yield is too low. The nominal yield is an important indicator for the level of share prices, and it shows the degree of acceptance by the investors of the value of the shares. In reality, the nominal yield from shares was once very high. For instance, on May 31, 1992, at the Shenzhen Stock Exchange the

annual highest nominal yield was for "Zhujiang" which stood at 176 and the lowest was for "Bao'an," at 33, while in deciding the issue price the nominal yield was calculated by multiplying by 15. It was far removed from the actual nominal yield and greatly underestimated the value of the shares, resulting in a strange phenomenon that, while the demand far outstripped the supply on the stock market, the price level remained low. This situation is not advantageous for the enterprises to make use of the capital market in reducing the cost of funds and effectively improves returns from the use of funds.

(2) The difference in issue prices is not wide enough. At the Shenzhen Stock Exchange, the gap in market prices is very wide — as high as 60 yuan per share for some shares and as low as 20 yuan for others. To a large extent, share prices have reflected the achievements of the enterprises. But, the issue price of most shares quoted on the Shenzhen Stock Exchange ranges between 2-4 yuan. This insignificant difference cannot accurately reflect the actual performance of the enterprises. Therefore, it inevitably results in a situation that all enterprises "eat from the same big pot" when it comes to the collection of funds. Thus, to exclusively decide the issue of prices on the basis of an estimated 15-fold nominal yield in disregard of the background and performance of the individual enterprises and industries is neither conducive to the enterprises making efforts to improve their management and increase returns nor instrumental for the stock market to fully play its role in guiding the flow of funds. Unified nominal yield is not beneficial for macroeconomic control by the state because it does not reflect the state's preferential policies towards key industries.

(3) The formula has not taken into consideration other related factors. The issue prices of shares differ from their market prices. The market prices always change along with changes in supply and demand, while the issue prices must remain stable within a period of time. Apart from taking into account of factors that cause fluctuations in share prices, consideration should also be given to such fundamental factors that affect the overall level of share prices as interest rates, inflation rates, the net value of

assets, and the influence of the level of returns and the risks on issue prices. The above formula failed to give consideration to these fundamental factors.

All this gives rise to an outstanding problem in China's stock market — a large price gap between the primary stock market and secondary market. Sometimes the market price is four or five times higher than the issue price. Consequently, huge profits derived from such a large price gap go to investors who bought the original issue shares, resulting in an excessive swelling of demand on the primary stock market. As for the secondary market, it is deprived of vitality because a lack of funds. Such a situation has seriously hindered the healthy development of China's stock market. It must be rectified.

When the demand for new issue shares far exceeds the supply, it is of vital importance to select an appropriate and reasonable model of issue for maintaining social order and preventing chaos. To limit the amount of underwriting application forms can produce a counter-reaction to the issue of new shares, as it elevates demand and price.

There are some difficulties in fixing share prices. First, it is difficult to decide the value of shares. As a monetary instrument, shares differ from commodities in kind. The value of commodities represents the value of material and labor used in producing them, while the value of shares is the expected dividend and the expected share appreciation. But, there are many factors that affect the dividend and the appreciation of shares, such as interest rates, risk factors and people's psyche. And some of these factors are hard to precisely pin down. This, in turn, makes it very difficult and complicated to decide the value of shares. Second, changes in share prices are irregular. Like commodities in kind, the prices of shares fluctuate around their value. But, the fluctuation of share prices is extremely irregular in terms of range and frequency, mainly because the share prices are affected not only by economic factors but also by political and psychological factors. Therefore, it is necessary to analyze the trend of price changes and accurately fix the issue prices of shares.

3. To Scientifically and Reasonably Fixing Share Issue Prices, It Is of Primary Importance to Analyze the Fundamental Factors That Affect Issue Prices; It Is Necessary to Employ Qualitative and Quantitative Methods in the Analysis and Forecast.

Factors that affect the issue prices are as follows:

The issue prices of shares are limited by the amount of capital. One of the characteristics of a shareholding company is that all its capital is divided into shares. Each represents a share of stockholder's right. The total sum of the nominal value of all of the company's shares equals its total capital. Issuing shares at a price lower than the nominal value will give a false picture of the company's total capital. Therefore, the share issue price is restricted by the amount of the company's capital. It must ensure that, when a certain portion of the shares are sold out, the company must obtain a corresponding amount of cash capital. This means that the issue price should in no way be lower than the nominal value.

The share issue price is conditioned by the net value of assets. As a token of investment, shares enable the shareholders to enjoy certain rights over the assets of an enterprise, and the rights are decided by the net value of assets the shares represent. Although the share price sometimes deviates from the net value of assets they represent, in the long run it should move in the same direction as the net value of assets it represents, that is, a share that represents greater net value of assets has a higher price.

The issue price should guarantee the integrity of the shareholders' rights. As many of the shareholding enterprises in China are developed from state-owned enterprises, shareholders representing the state should be given priority in subscribing to new shares in order to ensure that the value of state-owned assets is maintained and increased.

It is necessary to scientifically forecast the future returns of an enterprise. An important factor that affects the changes of share prices is how efficiently an enterprise is run. Therefore, it is imperative to make a comprehensive analysis of the enterprise in fixing a reasonable issue price for shares. The analysis should cover the following major aspects: (a) The competitive strength of the enterprise, mainly the volume, growth rate, stability and prospects of sales; (b) the capacity of the enterprise in earning profit, mainly the indexes of the rate of gross profit, the rate of capital turnover, the rate of profit from investment and the post-tax profit rate of each share; (c) the level of management proficiency in the enterprise, mainly production management, quality control, cost control and sales management; and (d) the financial condition of the enterprise, including the capital structure, ratio of liabilities to net worth and the guarantee of obligations. Only on the basis of such a comprehensive analysis of the enterprise can it be possible to scientifically forecast its returns and risks, and then reasonably decide the issue price of the shares.

It is necessary to decide reasonable rates of market gains. Judging from international experience, stock returns on stock markets in developed countries, which have developed into maturity and whose growth is slow and stable, are mainly from dividends. Hence, the nominal yield is comparatively low, normally ranging between 10 and 20 fold of the nominal value. In developing countries, stock markets are still in a stage of rapid growth: investment returns from shares are mainly from share premiums, and the nominal yield usually ranges between 20 and 30 fold. China's stock market is also in a stage of growth; therefore, it is necessary to adopt different rates of market gains in line with the specific conditions of different enterprises so as to place the determination of the issue prices of shares on a more scientific and reasonable basis.

It is necessary to attach importance to technical analysis of shares. The issue of shares is undertaken at a given time. The share price level at the time is an important factor affecting the success or failure of the issue. When the market is bullish, it will be easy to make the issue succeed; when the market is dull and demand dwindles, it will be difficult. Therefore, it will help to consciously decide the issue prices to ensure the success of an issue. This requires analyzing the trends and range of short-term price fluctuations on the stock market.

As the conditions in different regions, industries and companies vary greatly, it often necessary to decide an average premium level before deciding the premium level for each company, and then decide the corresponding premium levels in line with the specific conditions of different regions, industries and companies. The only standard in deciding the average premium level is the average nominal yield. The nominal yield obtained by dividing the market price of a share by its profit after tax. Why is it necessary to take the average nominal yield as the standard for deciding the average premium level? It is because, although share prices are affected by many factors, the fundamental and deciding factor is a company's ability to reap profits, i.e., the post-tax profit per share.

How is the average nominal yield decided? It must be decided in line with market supply and demand. Otherwise, it will make issue prices either too high or too low. To achieve this end, the average nominal yield on the secondary market can be applied directly. Yet, the average nominal yield on the issue market should be proportionately lower than that on the secondary market. This is because it takes some time from the issue of shares to their being quoted on the market, and during this time the shares lack mobility.

In addition, investors face the risk of price drops on the secondary market. As there is a certain gap in share price level between the Shenzhen Stock Exchange and the Shanghai Stock Exchange, it is therefore necessary to, when calculating the average nominal yield on the secondary market, add the nominal yield of the two stock exchanges and then divide it by two. To ensure a smooth issuing process, the nominal yield from which the issue price is determined should be 30 percent lower than the secondary market nominal yield. Moreover, since share prices on the secondary market frequently change, the average of the past three months should be used to figure out the average nominal yield on the secondary market. This will correct the influence accidental factors may have had on the share price.

Having decided the average nominal yield, work can then go on to decide the premium levels of shares issued by different companies in accordance with their specific conditions. In settling the premium levels for various companies, at least the following factors should be taken into consideration:

(1) Profit after tax per share in the coming three years. The

ability of a company to reap profit is the most important factor in deciding the share issue price. Because shares are tokens of ownership for unlimited periods of time, the shareholders cannot demand the company return their capital, yet they can receive dividends on their shares and enjoy certain rights over the remaining assets of the company. Therefore, the greater the ability of a company to reap profit, the higher its share value, and consequently, the higher the share issue price. The ability of a company to reap profit can be measured by the post-tax profit per share. To the shareholders, what is most important is also the post-tax profit per share. As it is rather difficult to make long-term forecasts and it is necessary to take into consideration the announcements usually made by China's shareholding companies in forecasting their post-tax profits for a three-year period; the three-year post-tax profit per share of a company is therefore extremely important in deciding its premium level.

(2) The risk level. Risks encountered by a company in its management are also an important factor affecting the price of its shares. The higher the risks, the lower the price of the shares. Risks can be categorized into five classes: high, modestly high, medium, modestly low, and low. Risks are calculated in line with state industry policies for the specific industry to which a company belongs, their composition of assets, financial strength and the degree of diversification of their operations as well as historical factors. The five classes of risks can then be quantified into risk coefficients 0.5, 0.75, 1, 1.25 and 1.5. The smaller the risk coefficient, the lower the degree of risk.

(3) The factors for readjustment. To decide the value of the factors for readjustment, it is necessary to take into account the following factors: 1) The assessment method of intangible assets. When shifting to the shareholding system, various places have adopted different methods in assessing such intangible assets as the right to use land, patents and commercial credit. Some have included the entire value of the intangible assets in the total net value of the company; others included part and still other has not included it at all. Experts hold that, for businesses which included only part or none of the value of the intangible assets in their total

net asset value, the value of the factors for readjustment should be made proportionately higher so as to raise the issue price of shares. 2) Long-term investment. When turning into the share-holding system, various places have also adopted different methods in assessing the long-term investment of the company. Some have assessed the value of the investment on the basis of their current real worth, while others have calculated it according to the book value. If calculated according to the book value, it is then necessary to readjust the issue price of shares by altering the value of factors for readjustment in line with such factors as the duration of the long-term investment by the company, and the returns and appreciation of such investment. 3) The portion of new issue shares in the original issue shares. The higher the portion of new issue shares, the lower the issue price should be. 4) The method of converting the net assets of the company into shares. When converting the net assets of a company into shares, companies in most places have converted the *assessed* net value of the company's assets into shares with equal value, while Shanghai and a few other places based the share value on *book value* of the company's net assets. As a result, the premium level in Shanghai is relatively higher. According to the various situations described above, we may set the value of the factors for readjustment at 0-2, with the median value at 1.

Monetary experts have quantified the above-mentioned factors and assigned them, according to their importance, weighted values ranging from 15 percent to 25 percent (the weighted values should add up to "1"), and hence proposed the following formula to calculate the premium level:

$$P = (K1 \times a \times 25\% + K2 \times a \times 20\% + K3 \times a \times 15\%) + (K1 \times a \times r \times 20\%) + (K1 \times a \times b \times 20\%)$$

In the formula, "P" represents the stock issue price; "K1," "K2" and "K3" represent the post-tax profit in the first, second and third years respectively, the post-tax profit refers to profit after deducting income tax, the contributions to funds not covered by state budget and the contributions to funds for constructing transport facilities; "a" means nominal yield **I**, which is the average of nominal yield **I** of all shares quoted at the Shanghai and Shenzhen stock exchanges in the last three months; "r" indicates the risk coefficient; and "b" is the coefficient of readjustment.

For instance, a company is reshuffled into a limited-liability company and plans to issue common shares, each with a nominal value of one yuan. The post-tax profit for each of the company's shares in the next three years is expected to be 0.15 yuan, 0.25 yuan and 0.40 yuan respectively. The average nominal yield **I** at the Shanghai and Shenzhen stock exchanges over the last three months is 30-fold. The department in charge rated the company's risk class as intermediate, that is, its risk coefficient is 1. The coefficient of readjustment is 1.5. So, the issue price of the company's shares is:

$$P = (0.15 \times 30 \times 25\% + 0.25 \times 30 \times 20\% + 0.40 \times 30 \times 15\%)$$
$$+ (0.15 \times 30 \times 1 \times 20\%) + (0.15 \times 30 \times 1.5 \times 20\%)$$
$$= 6.675 \text{ (yuan)}$$

In Western countries, the issue of shares is underwritten by securities houses. The issue price is decided through negotiations between the issuing companies and the underwriting companies on the basis of the nominal yield. But, in some countries, if the shares underwritten to the securities houses do not sell well, they must be sold at reduced prices. Therefore, deciding the issue price holds great risks for securities houses.

One important difference between the shareholding system being introduced on a trial basis in China and the shareholding economy practised in Western countries is that China introduces the shareholding system on the basis of state-owned enterprises (including, of course, enterprises under other types of ownership); the former company's stock is not sold, rather new shares are issued to the public.

Since China's stock market has just been established, the laws and regulations concerning the stock market still leave much to be desired. The accounting system still has a long way to go to reach international standards and the overall supply of shares usually falls short of demand. It is hard to establish a standard restraining mechanism for affixing the share prices. The companies that issue shares always hope to get higher premiums, and the securities houses, to solicit business, tend to offer higher underwriting prices because they do not have to worry about the buyers, and if they cannot sell the shares right away, they can keep them for the time being. However, higher issue prices inevitably create difficulties for the secondary market, and so there must be a relevant department that is responsible for securities affairs to check issue prices. This situation is unique to China's still-developing stock market.

Take Shanghai for example. The prices of shares quoted on the Shanghai Stock Exchange in 1992 were decided by the issuing companies and securities underwriting houses and reported to the Administrative Department of the People's Bank for checking. For its part, the People's Bank first calculated the post-tax profit per share on the basis of the profit rate provided by accounting firms at the end of 1991 and the expected rate in 1992, and used it to determine an appropriate nominal yield (which is decided according to the international convention that the nominal yield for industrial companies is relatively lower and nominal yield for tertiary companies is proportionately higher) to obtain the issue prices. These prices were then discussed again with the issuing companies and underwriting houses. Experts hold that this method of fixing issue prices in Shanghai is appropriate for the current development of China's stock market.

Section 4   The Problems of Mutual Funds and Internal Shares

1. The Birth and Development of Mutual Funds.

In the world, investment funds or trusts have many names. In the United States, they are called "mutual funds," while in Britain they are called "unit trusts." Investment funds are a popular instrument for securities investment. They are established by pooling the small amounts of money in the hands of ordinary people and investing it in various kinds of securities by commissioned investment experts in accordance with the principle of risk distribution. The returns are shared in proportion to the level of investment.

Investment funds have a fairly long history. They first appeared in Britain in the mid-19th century. At that time, Britain established its leading position as an industrial country, its domestic wealth increased rapidly. Because domestic interest rates went down, many medium and small investors vied with one another to invest their money in the United States and other countries with the aim of reaping more profits. Yet, they suffered losses because they were not familiar with the situation of overseas enterprises. Hence came into being the investment funds which were much appreciated by medium and small investors. The system was gradually introduced to other countries in Europe and the United States.

After World War II, the securities investment fund business developed very rapidly in various countries, and the variety and management of such funds continuously improved. Led by the United States, mutual funds came into vogue on stock markets in developed countries at the end of the 1970s. Since the 1980s, large amounts of capital have flowed from developed countries into the Asia-Pacific developing countries through these funds. At present, investment funds have become the most common way to make overseas securities investments.

The United States is the most developed in terms of the investment fund market: the total amount of mutual funds in the country reaches thousands of billions dollars, exceeding the total amount of savings deposits in all of its banks. Hong Kong has only a population of 6 million, yet there are about 1,000 varieties of mutual funds. In the United States, people joining such mutual funds account for 8 percent of its population; in Japan, 10 percent; in Britain, 4 percent; and in Hong Kong, 1 percent. Investment funds have become an important pattern of investment in many countries and regions.

In terms of organization, investment funds can be divided

into two types — the corporation type and the contractual type. By corporation type, it means raising funds by issuing shares through established shareholding investment companies. The characteristics are: the fund itself is a shareholding investment company; the investors are the company's shareholders; and the charter of the company clearly specifies the rights and obligations of the company and the shareholders. In the United States, most such funds are of the corporation type.

Contractual investment funds raise funds through trust agreements, which are signed by the fund management companies (securities investment and trust company) and the custodian companies of the funds (monetary organizations). The fund management companies act as the consignors of the agreements to decide the amount of the fund, are responsible for establishing the operation principles and are in charge of routine management of the fund; the custodian companies act as the trust executors of the agreement and are responsible for the safety and disposal of the assets of the fund. In such trust agreements, three parties are involved, namely, the consignors (managerial organs of the assets of the fund), fund executors (the custodians of the assets) and beneficiaries (the investors); the operation of the fund assets and the rights and obligations of all parties are defined by trust agreements. The contractual type of investment funds are adopted in most countries and regions, including Japan, Singapore and China's Taiwan Province.

In addition, investment funds are divided into two types, according to whether they can be expanded or not — the open-end type and the closed-end type. For open-end investment funds, the number of shares are not limited; new shares can be issued continuously to attract new investors. When investors wish to quit from the funds, the funds can buy back their shares. With closed-end funds, the number of shares are limited and no new shares can be issued after a pre-set period of time; investors cannot return the shares they hold but can trade them on the market. Judging by the current situation in the world, open-end investments trusts have been developing quickly. In the United States, over 90 percent of the investment companies are of the open-end type. In Taiwan, Singapore, Hong Kong and other developing countries and regions, open-end investment companies also make up a very large proportion.

2. The Advantages of Mutual Funds: Accessible to Small Investors, Dispersion of Risks, Professional Management and Desirable Returns.

Compared with other monetary assets, investment funds have unique advantages.

(1) They are accessible to small investors and conducive to pooling idle funds in society. Be it in developed countries or developing ones, the majority of people have only a moderate amount of savings and cannot make major investments in the stock market. Investment funds, however, are calculated according to the purchased units or shares, and each is only several yuan or several dozen yuan, accessible to all investors. Hence, they are an ideal monetary tool for China's wage-earning class. In addition, government employees and employees in the securities business can make indirect investment in shares through choosing the right investment funds, thus making it possible to pool social idle funds from a wider range.

(2) They make it possible to disperse investment risk. Normally, diversifying the composition of an investment portfolio disperses the risk. This is precisely the strong point of investment funds. They have abundant amounts of money and can invest in an ever wider range of securities simultaneously. Losses in one area can be offset by gains in another, ensuring relatively stable and safe returns.

(3) Investment funds are professionally managed by monetary experts at specialized investment institutions. These experts are familiar with the securities industry, well informed and equipped with advanced telecommunications means. Therefore, they are more likely to make correct decisions than individual investors.

(4) The cash flow and realization are better. People have to consider three factors in making any investment — profitability, safety and liquidity. Since they can be bought or sold any time,

investment funds have good liquidity.

(5) The cost is low. People with a great amount of money can hire professional investment advisors to take care of their invested assets. This practice, however, is beyond the grasp of medium and small investors; to get this level of service, they have to invest their money in investment funds. In this way, all people who put their money with the funds share the management costs of the investment trust companies while enabling their invested assets to enjoy professional management. In addition, the investment trust companies, as professional investment companies, can make large deals on the stock exchanges, thus reducing the share transaction cost and investment cost, bringing the investors better gains.

(6) The returns are considerable. Returns from investment funds are composed of three parts, namely, income from interests, income from dividends and capital revenue (money earned from buying and selling securities). Judging by the current management and financial status of the listed enterprises in China as well as quotations of the listed shares and bonds, as long as the investment funds are properly managed, they are able to produce considerable returns. In addition, investors can acquire capital revenue through buying and selling their shares — buying when the prices are low and selling when the prices rise.

3. Developing Investment Funds in China Is Conducive to the Healthy Growth of the Stock Market, to the Development of New Financial Products and to Opening Up New Fund-Raising Channels.

A developed and mature stock market is indispensable to the development of the socialist market economy. Vigorous efforts in developing investment funds can release the potential of the stock market. In addition, investment trust companies, in order to reap long-term returns, are more likely to make objective and rational investment decisions rather than make speculations on the market; this is beneficial to achieving a balance between the market supply and demand and can promote the healthy and well-coordinated development of China's stock market.

The development of investment funds opens up a new channel for raising capital and adds vitality to China's economic development. As the most basic social resources in economic life and the most important production factor for enterprises, funds have been in short supply for a long time in China. The development of the capital market broadens enterprises' channel to raise funds, promotes the conversion of idle funds into investment, thus adding sustained vitality to the economic development.

The development of investment funds is conducive to the creation of new financial instruments and can satisfy people's diversified demands for financial assets. The development of the stock market calls for the diversification of securities tools. The vigorous development of investment funds can increase the variety of securities and promote monetary innovation, thus producing a wider and more effective appeal to investors and enhancing the potential for the development of the stock market.

The development of investment trusts is advantageous to attracting overseas investments. Investment trusts hold appeal to overseas investors because: 1) The overseas investments brought in by the investment funds enter China in the form of equity capital, and it only needs to remit the dividends, interests and capital revenue abroad, which does not increase the country's debt burden; 2) the risks of interest rate and exchange rate fluctuations are born by the overseas investors, thus sparing China losses caused by setting an improper value for the currency when borrowing loans from other countries; 3) overseas investment brought in by the investment funds are indirect investments, which are not aimed at controlling the enterprises or the market and, moreover, do not cause competition with China's relevant industries, thus avoiding the drawbacks in bringing in direct investments by overseas investors.

The investment funds make it possible for government employees and other wage-earners to make investment in securities (particularly in shares) and prevent government officials from abusing their power for personal gain. At present, the government rules that Party and government officials are not allowed to buy shares; the purpose is to prevent them from abusing their power for personal gain and intervening in market activities. The prohibition covers so wide a range that it cannot possibly be implemented. Besides, it seems inappropriate to rob the Party and government officials of the right to invest.

At the same time, investment funds can help turn individual investments by wage-earners into investments by legal entities and help them avoid some practical problems encountered when they make direct investments. For instance, it is impossible for Party and government officials and some other wage-earners to have enough time to observe and study stock market trends and to select the right investment opportunities.

In sum, mutual funds are an collective investment model that can achieve common prosperity, and are in accord with the principles of China's socialist system.

4. To Develop Mutual Funds in China, It Is Necessary to Pay Full Attention to the Problem of Standardization and Strengthen Supervision and Control.

Because investment funds are an investment model characterized by "popular raising of funds, expert management and collective benefits," and because investment funds are a form of fund raising that is highly specialized and produces a wide range of influence, full emphasis should be attached to their standardization while active experiments are conducted. The establishment of such funds must be subject to examination and approval by the departments in charge and any "underground funds" should be banned.

At the same time, it is necessary to establish and improve the public information-disclosure system. When issuing fund shares, the investment trust companies must announce publicly their programs or trust agreements. In addition, they should give public notice at regular intervals regarding the net value of their assets and the utilization of the assets, so as to effectively guarantee the interests of the investors.

So far, China has not established a comprehensive fund market and fund administrative system. Nevertheless, it is imperative to attach importance to the role and significance of supervision and control of the fund market. All other countries enforce very strict and standard control over investment funds; they all have enacted special legislation concerning the control of the investment activities of the trusts. The *Investment Company Act* adopted by the United States in 1940 is a special law governing investment funds. Like the *Securities Act*, adopted in 1933, and the *Securities Exchange Act*, adopted in 1934, the *Investment Company Act* is also an important legislation governing the stock market. In Japan, the relevant laws include the *Securities Investment Act*, adopted in 1948, *Securities Trust Act*, adopted in 1951, and *Amendment to the Securities Trust Act*, adopted in 1967. In Hong Kong, apart from control by the securities and futures control authorities, investment trust administrative committee has also established such autonomous organizations as the Unit Trust Committee and Unit Trust Fund. At present, China's administrative work concerning investment funds are still confined to local provisions. In June 1992, Shenzhen promulgated *Provisional Regulations Concerning the Administration Over Investment Trust Funds*. Departments concerned should work out legislation on the administration of investment funds as soon as possible so as to make the development of China's investment funds along a standard orbit.

The development of investment funds and the development of securities business rely on each other. At present, the variety of securities on the market is rather monotonous, and so the investment funds have a limited range of choice for investment and their advantages cannot be brought into full play. In addition, when the choices for investment are limited, there is the possibility for investment funds to become the major buyers on the stock market and hence become a new force manipulating the stock market.

Judging by the current situation on China's investment fund market, there are still many practices which are not standard. For instance, some trust organizations have not clearly stated their organizational form — whether they are corporation or contractual; some do not have a trust executors system and name their own monetary organizations as the custodians of funds, make it impossible to exercise supervision over their operation; and still some even publicly announce in their notices their expected rates of returns. For the investors, investing in investment trusts are the same as investing in other forms: they must shoulder some risks (such as poor returns from the performance of the funds and fraudulent conducts on the part of the trust companies and the trusters). Therefore, it is urgently needed to publicize basic knowledge about investment funds.

In developing investment funds, it is necessary to make a choice between the open-end type and the closed-end type. In the past, China once tried out the closed-end type. The result was not satisfactory. It seems that China should find a way between the open-end and the closed-end types, as it is in conformity with China's reality.

Now, a new trend has appeared on the international stock market with regard to stock mix: The proportion held by individual investors has been coming down while that held by institutional investors has been on the rise. On developed stock market, institutional investors normally account for 50-60 percent. In Japan, corporate investors constitute 70-80 percent. On the stock market in Singapore, institutional investors make up about 80 percent, and they include trust funds, retirement pension funds, mutual aid funds and insurance companies. In China's Taiwan, however, individual investors account for a major proportion, around 80 percent. Therefore, some experts in Taiwan held that the low percentage of institutional investors and high percentage of individual investors are an important factor causing instability of Taiwan's stock market. In order to stabilize the stock market, one of the major measures adopted by the authorities in charge is to establish investment funds to raise funds, turn individual investments into corporate investments, and invest the money on the stock market. Yet, the net worth of the securities investment funds accounts for only 2.7 percent of the total market value of all shares listed on Taiwan's stock exchange now. In the developed countries of Europe and America, it accounts for around 20 percent. To promote the development of securities investment funds, the authorities in charge of securities industry in Taiwan approved the establishment of 11 securities investment and trust companies in 1992 alone.

With regard to the stock mix on China's stock market, on the one hand, the proportion of state shares to corporate shares is too large, and on the other, the majority of shares traded on the market are personal shares. Such a lopsided stock mix has led to a lopsided development of the stock market. Hence, adjusting the stock mix is crucial for promoting the normal development of the stock market. It should include the following aspects:

— Reduce the proportion of state shares by varying degrees for different industries and enterprises.

— Actively develop contractual savings organizations such as pension funds, and allow them to enter the capital market and invest certain portions of their assets on the stock market (in line with the principles for safe and sound investment) so as to increase the proportion of institutional investors on the stock market.

— Develop mutual funds to turn individual investments into corporate investments. The money of the investment funds can be invested on the stock market or the market for bonds.

5. Strengthening Management of Internal Shares.

In some countries, there are two situations in which the workers and staff of given companies hold shares of their own companies: those companies that are listed on the market and those that are not listed. With listed companies, the workers and staff holding their shares enjoy the same rights as other investors and the shares they hold can be traded on the stock market. With unlisted companies, internal shares issued to their own workers and staff cannot be transferred on the stock market but only among the workers and staff of the companies at the nominal value of the shares; and the companies are responsible to complete the formalities of the transfers. Usually, the unlisted shares issued by companies serve only as a transition. Once the companies are listed, the formerly unlisted shares can now be listed and traded on the market. Often, it takes a certain period of time, normally three years, from the issue of such internal shares to their being listed on the stock market.

For a certain period, many problems appeared in the issue of internal shares by companies not listed in various places. First, the so-called internal shares went beyond their limits and were issued to all individuals who wished to buy. Second, the trading of such shares was not limited to the workers and staff of the companies either; they could be sold and bought by anyone; and their prices were decided by market demand and supply. This in fact was a type of black market trading.

As both the issue and trading of such shares are not conducted according to pertinent laws and regulations, the rights and interests of the investors cannot be guaranteed and there are many loopholes for unlawful speculators. Their unchecked development is bound to interrupt the normal order of the stock market and undermine its sound development. This question has aroused the attention of departments in charge of the stock market and certain measures have been taken.

First of all, efforts have been made to correct the one-sided view that it is "safer" to issue internal shares than publicly issue shares in society. Because of this, the control over public issue of shares was very strict while that over issue of internal shares was loose, resulting in overissuing of internal shares. In 1992, the total nominal value of internal shares, including personal shares and corporate shares, issued by various companies throughout the country exceeded 10 billion yuan (around 2 billion yuan for personal shares). At the same time, it was made clear that the holding of shares by workers and staff of limited-liability companies should only be treated as a transitional form before the companies' shares are listed on the stock market; they should never be treated as a parallel form of public issue of shares in society.

Second, policies of persuasion have been adopted along with policies of strict control, and controlled quotas of public issue of shares for various localities were appropriately adjusted. Because of the strict control over public issue of shares, some regions, where the adoption of the shareholding system have proceeded more rapidly, were compelled to use the issue of so-called internal shares to replace the public issue of shares in society. Therefore, it is necessary to enforce strict and regular control and supervision over the issue and transfer of internal shares. In order to stop the wanton issue of internal shares and black market practices, the internal shares can be allowed to be issued without notes, that is, just issuing the certificates which are put on record by the companies. The transfer of such shares among the workers and staff in the companies can be handled by special organizations set up by the companies.

Chapter 3
The Stock Trading Market and
Its Regulation

Section 1 Gradation and Distribution of China's Stock Trading Market

1. How to Make the Gradation and Distribution of China's Stock Trading Market More Scientific and Rational.

So far, a pattern that combines concentrated and scattered trading characterizes China's stock trading market. The concentrated trading market comprises two exchanges, two systems and three centers. The two exchanges are the Shanghai Stock Exchange and the Shenzhen Stock Exchange; the two systems are the National Securities Trading Automated Quotation System (STAQ) and the National Electronic Trading System (NET); and the three centers are the Tianjin Securities Trading Center, the Wuhan Securities Trading Center and the Shenyang Securities Trading Center. Listed on the two stock exchanges are mainly personal shares issued by the quoted companies; the STAQ and NET systems in Beijing simultaneously handle the trial circulation of state treasury bonds and corporate shares; the three securities centers mainly deal with transactions in state treasury bonds and investment funds.

The market for scattered trading refers to the more than 3,000 securities concerns throughout the country, including securities houses, securities offices run by trust companies as well as securities offices of banks and credit cooperatives, which mainly handle over-the-counter transactions in bonds.

Experts in theoretical circles and in the field have been speculating about whether China's stock trading market system can keep pace with the development of China's stock market, whether it is necessary to establish a third stock exchange, and whether it is necessary to open more places where medium-sized and small companies can raise funds. Some people hold that, in line with China's reality, it is necessary to establish a securities trading network that comprises three levels.

At the first level would be the national trading centers. For instance, Shanghai can be treated as the national trading center and Shenzhen can be looked on as the national trading center for B shares. At the second level would be local stock exchanges in some major cities — control over enterprises quoted at these exchanges can be less strict. The third level would be over-the-counter trading in medium-sized cities.

The major arguments for establishing such a three-level national securities trading network are as follows:

(1) China has a vast territory, the number of enterprises is gigantic and the conditions in quoted enterprises vary greatly. If the trading is concentrated in one or two stock exchanges, the pressure will be onerous and the actual operation would not be easy. In this respect, China is not like Singapore and Hong Kong where concentrated trading is much easier.

(2) China's stock market is still in its early stages of development. Normally, trading at developmental stages is scattered and is then gradually concentrated. Yet, the concentration takes time.

(3) Shareholders in China do not have sufficient knowledge of the situation on the stock market and of quoted companies. It takes time for shareholders to get to know the companies and it is also necessary for shareholders to supervise the companies' activities. If the trading is over-concentrated, it will be impossible for the shareholders to acquire sufficient information about quoted companies and difficult for them to exercise their supervisory right. In view of China's reality, a multi-level market is advantageous for shareholders to gain access to information about and exercise supervision over the companies.

(4) The companies and shares in China are of different types; for instance, quoted companies and internal companies, personal shares and corporate shares, as well as A and B shares — and

possibly C shares — in the future. Therefore, it might be better to establish a market which is divided into several levels, each of which handles the circulation of a particular variety of shares.

Looking at the growth of stock markets in developing countries around the world, we see a common pattern: the market is at first scattered and it gradually becomes concentrated and unified. Experts hold that this is the normal pattern of development. Then, how many stock exchanges should be established? One to two? Or six to 12 as in some other countries?

In China, the establishment of an ideal national stock trading market must be a gradual process because remote areas lack a well-developed telecommunications network. Russia at present is an example of the extreme. In name, there are several dozen stock exchanges, in addition to several hundred that consider themselves stock exchanges. In fact, there are only few which can really be called stock exchanges. In their operation, these so-called stock exchanges have formed their own rules and systems.

The best way is to establish just a few rather than several dozen or a hundred stock exchanges. In addition, they should only be established in major cities. The trading principles, management rules, operational mechanism and trading procedures of these exchanges should all be the same. On this basis, a national trading market could be gradually established.

To view it from another angle, although the trading systems in other countries have gone from being scattered to being concentrated, it does not necessarily mean that China must also go through this process. This is because the establishment of a multi-level trading network demands that the service organizations, such as the liquidation companies, clearing houses and registration houses, all be on several levels, thus resulting in great waste. In addition, the establishment of a trading network calls for large investment of funds, which is a burden impossible for any local government to bear, and the quick training of needed personnel. Therefore, establishing a large number of stock exchanges does not conform to China's reality.

Some other people argue that the current national stock circulation market based on the two stock exchanges in Shanghai and Shenzhen has already been insufficient to meet the needs of the development of the joint-stock economy, and that China must urgently establish a third stock exchange. They recommend that the third stock exchange be established in Wuhan.

The history of development of the market economy over the past few centuries indicates that the joint-stock companies and the stock market are twin babies that exist and flourish side by side, and it is impossible for the joint-stock economy to flourish without a developed stock market. The success or failure of the stock market not only relies on this market observing the general laws of the stock market but also depends on whether or not a market system suited to China's actual conditions is established. In this sense, the stock market systems in Western countries are not entirely identical. The United States has a system which comprises seven major stock exchanges and one invisible network; Japan has six stock exchanges distributed from the north to the south while the Tokyo Stock Exchange includes in itself an invisible network; and most medium-sized and small countries in Europe have one stock exchange or several stock exchanges.

China has a vast territory and large population, and transport and telecommunications are underdeveloped. In addition, the economic conditions in the major economic zones differ greatly. The issue whether the establishment of a nationally unified stock market can comply with the realities of China certainly warrants study. Some people suggest establishing stock exchanges in the major economic zones. Of course, the establishment in these major economic zones must also implemented in separate steps in line with the different conditions of market development. As the waves of reform and opening to the outside world surge towards the hinterland of the country, it is particularly necessary to establish stock exchanges in the interior.

The 14th National Congress of the Communist Party of China mapped out a strategy to shift the focus of reform and opening to the outside world from the coastal areas to areas along the Yangtze River and border areas. Since then, some inland cities have opened their doors wide to the outside world. Yet, the stock market, which is considered the hallmark of reform and opening to the outside world, is still limited to the coastal areas. In fact, international financial centers in other countries are not necessarily limited to coastal cities. For instance, Chicago in the United States, Birmingham in Britain, Paris and Leone in France, Frankfurt in Germany, Zurich in Switzerland and Milan in Italy are all inland cities. Yet, they are world-known financial centers. The establishment of stock exchanges in some key inland cities, if accomplished, not only means going along with the international trend but will also help implement the Party Central Committee's strategic decision to shift the focus of reform and opening to inland areas.

The development of the Shanghai and Shenzhen stock exchanges shows that the establishment of stock exchanges can play an extremely important role in regulating the conduct of the quoted companies, strengthening the market mechanism for enterprises and correctly guiding the investment activities of shareholders. Therefore, stock exchanges are not merely a pure trading instrument. More important, it is an administrative instrument. Through it, the government can most effectively control the stock market. In one sense, the establishment of a new stock exchange can alleviate the pressure on the Shanghai and Shenzhen stock exchanges. At the same time, it makes it possible to adopt suitable measures for the management, guidance and development of the stock market in line with particular local conditions.

Wuhan is one of China's largest metropolitan areas, a well-known and important industrial city and also one of the cities picked by the state to try out economic, financial and scientific and technological reforms. In 1992, it was approved by the State Council as an open city along the Yangtze River. A securities network has taken shape in the city: there are at present over 100 securities houses, more than in any other city. Over the past few years, the total value of its securities transactions has been second only to Shanghai. In 1992, its total volume of business in state treasury bonds reached 16 billion yuan, outstripping Shanghai, to become No. 1 in the country.

In addition, Wuhan has a site for concentrated trading in securities — the Wuhan Securities Trading Center, which is surpassed only by the Shanghai and Shenzhen stock exchanges in scale. Now, the center has more than 100 members from 15 provinces, municipalities and autonomous regions; its daily, weekly and annual volume of business in state treasury bonds tops any other city, thus making it the biggest trading market in state treasury bonds in China. In addition, it is equipped with advanced computers and other trading facilities and employs international stock exchange management and operation standards. Therefore, some experts hold that the conditions are ripe for a Wuhan stock exchange.

2. Over-the-Counter Transactions Are Necessary at the Current Stage. Yet, Their Development Is Conditional.

The establishment of a multi-level trading system conforms to China's reality. This is because China has a large territory, the economic development is uneven and the entire enterprise setup is characterized by small, independent businesses. Each of China's provinces is as large as a major European country. If the shares of all quoted companies are traded in Shanghai and Shenzhen, it is bound to be very inconvenient for either the quoted companies and trading companies or the investors. Moreover, along with the development of joint-stock system, a mammoth amount of internal shares needs to be circulated and transferred. Over-the-counter transactions can meet such needs.

The market for over-the-counter transactions is a component of the stock market. The reasons for its existence and development are: it can provide a channel and a trading platform for those medium-sized and small companies which issue shares but cannot be quoted; in addition, it provides a grand marketing network for securities with sound credit (listed shares issued by large companies and government bonds).

Take the situation in Thailand for example. There are various types of sites for over-the-counter transactions. Technically, Thailand adopts the British over-the-counter market model, or "organized over-the-counter trading." About six years ago, the Thailand Stock Exchange came to realize that, if only one stock exchange was in operation, the conditions for companies wishing to be quoted would be very rigid, and this makes it impossible for the numerous medium-sized and small companies to raise funds through the stock market. It was decided to establish an over-the-counter trading market. Hence, two types of stock exchanges independent of each other appeared: One was for listing shares issued by companies that have sound operation records, and the other was for trading in shares or bonds issued by companies that have operated less successfully (their profit record may not be as sound as companies in the first category), or they are small in size and fail to reach certain standards. Based on such considerations, an over-the-counter market was established several years ago in Thailand, and it has proven successful in giving medium-sized businesses increased fund-raising opportunities.

The over-the-counter market can make up for certain drawbacks of stock exchanges; and, as the trading on such markets are characterized by simplicity and flexibility, it has become an indispensable and important part of the stock market. Over-the-counter trading must possess the following two conditions:

(1) The prices must be unified throughout the country.

(2) Every kind of securities quoted can be easily bought and sold over the counter throughout the country.

To meet the two conditions, it is necessary to have a well-developed telecommunications system and a well-developed information disclosure system so that investors all over the country can buy and sell shares and bonds with the same prices at the counters everywhere.

The example of Shenzhen is illustrative. Before the Shenzhen Stock Exchange was established, there were over a dozen over-the-counter markets in the city alone. In front of every counter, people queued up for consignment purchases and sales, including opening entries, deposits of securities and registration. In fact, each counter acted as a small stock exchange. The drawbacks of over-the-counter trading in Shenzhen at that time were typical.

(1) The price signals are not unified. People encountered many different prices as at many markets. For instance, the price for the Development Bank stock might be 11 yuan at one counter, 12 yuan at the second one and 13 yuan at a third one. This

provides an opportunity for some investors to speculate by taking advantage of price differentials.

(2) Unfair practices by people working at the counters can easily occur. Over-the-counter transactions do not have a time sequence. Because of this, friends and relatives of these people can conclude deals on the side, without having stood in the queue. Moreover, it is impossible to enforce effective supervision over such market manipulative practices, for over-the-counter transactions are not like deals made in stock exchanges which must be sequentially entered into computers.

(3) Open over-the-counter trading can easily lead to local fragmentation. For instance, if over-the-counter trading is introduced in Wuhan, the local government in the city, in order to make the local trading prosperous, will be reluctant to allow the companies in the city to trade their shares in Shenzhen and Shanghai. Conversely, it will also be possible for Shenzhen and Shanghai to be unwilling to accept companies from other places. This will finally result in local embargoes.

Consequently, to establish scattered trading markets in haste when the conditions are not ripe could give rise to many problems. But, when the telecommunications system is well-developed and a normal channel of information disclosure has been opened, there will be no need for such scattered trading markets.

Some experts hold that all other countries have traversed such a course of development, that is, from being scattered to being concentrated, in the development of their securities trading networks. It warrants earnest study whether it is imperative that China must also go through this process, or whether it is possible for it to bypass this process, in the development of its own securities trading network.

Some other experts argue that both national and local stock exchanges should be allowed to grow naturally and gradually.

3. International Experience to Be Learned.

Judging by the situation of a few major stock markets in the United States, Japan and elsewhere, the stock exchange is the most common organizational form of the stock market. Stock exchanges are divided into three levels — national stock exchanges, local stock exchanges and over-the-counter markets. For the United States and Japan, this pattern of setup was not deliberately established; it has evolved into the current multi-level pattern for various reasons. In the United States, the New York Stock Exchange and the American Stock Exchange are of unique significance and are regarded as national stock exchanges because they are the biggest in terms of the volume of business and because they cover the entire country in terms of business range. Compared with the American Stock Exchange, the New York Stock Exchange is far larger in business, the number of companies quoted and the number of members. Apart from these two, there are another six or seven local stock exchanges. To say they are local, it mainly means that the companies quoted at these stock exchanges are basically local companies, which, when compared with those national companies, are somewhat inferior in terms of achievements, assets and amount of shares traded on the market.

Next comes the over-the-counter market. In the United States, it refers to the National Association of Securities Dealers Automated Quotation (NASDAQ). In historical terms, this system is a low-level trading market. It mainly provides opportunities for small companies to raise funds; it is flexible and not so strict in managerial and institutional terms compared with national stock exchanges.

With regard to the current structure of secondary trading market, over-the-counter market in Japan has withered and its function for companies to raise funds has been replaced by stock exchanges. NASD in the United States is the only case of development; it shows a trend of outstripping the New York Stock Exchange in both the volume of business and the quality of quoted companies. The United States is also the most successful in establishing the best and most vigorous organizational form for over-the-counter trading. One cannot find a well-established over-the-counter market in Europe and other parts of the world.

Usually in the United States, when a company is small, it raises funds on the over-the-counter market; when it grows to a certain size, it goes to the local stock exchange to raise funds; and when the scale and circulation of its assets and the number of shareholders further develop, it could be quoted on the American Stock Exchange and finally it may turn to the New York Stock Exchange for funds. In terms of organizational form, the secondary market is divided into the three levels; each level has its unique functions and serves as the site for a certain group of companies to raise funds.

Trading in securities is normally divided into two categories: floor transactions, i.e., transactions within the stock exchanges, and over-the-counter transactions. The advanced over-the-counter market is composed of computerized automated quotation system. In many countries, the setup of stock exchanges falls into three categories. The first is the coexistence of national and local stock exchanges. Take the United States for example. There are nine major stock exchanges, of which three are national: the New York Stock Exchange, the American Stock Exchange and the Chicago Stock Exchange. The rest are local stock exchanges. The second type is that all stock exchanges are local. For instance, the 13 stock exchanges in India are all local ones. The third type is that there is only one or two national stock exchanges. Most developing countries fall into this category.

In countries like the United States, the development of a securities exchange system has traversed a long course. Although the New York Stock Exchange developed continuously, activities at other securities centers throughout the country long remained separated and their trading in securities bore a strong local mark due to the influence of technology and other factors. In 1975, a national securities exchange act was adopted. Since then, securities institutions have made extensive use of computers and other new equipment, greatly raising the efficiency and capacity of securities exchange. The most significant step was the merger of the New York Stock Exchange and the Pacific Stock Exchange (on the west coast). In this way, when the New York Stock Exchange is closed, its business can be carried on immediately at the Pacific Stock Exchange (which stays open three hours later due to the time difference), thus combining the securities business on the east and west coasts into an organic whole.

At the initial stages in the development of a stock market, several stock exchanges usually exist side by side in many countries and regions; they will eventually merge into one, such as in Hong Kong and the Republic of Korea. The stock exchanges in the Philippines are also in the process of being merged. One important reason here is the lack of people who have intimate knowledge of the stock market and people who can perform supervisory and administrative duties over the stock market. In order to eliminate deals by insiders and market manipulation, it is extremely important to have sufficient well-trained supervisory and administrative personnel.

Moreover, as the technology to run a national unified stock market has been developed, there is no need to establish numerous stock exchanges. The problem encountered by many stock exchanges is that information is not disclosed promptly and sufficiently. Information disclosure is an important factor for the sound growth of the stock market, particularly so in China which has so many provinces. It is important for people to be able to simultaneously obtain accurate financial information about listed companies. So, it is necessary to establish a state-of-the-art information service system.

Another important aspect is the standardization of information, which is in a sense related to the internationalization of the stock market. Therefore, some people say that the development of a national market is the direction, yet the establishment of an ideal national stock exchange cannot but be gradual.

Yet, some experts have a different viewpoint. They contend that it is not necessarily correct that every country strives to build a national unified stock exchange. They argue that the same situation is not limited to the monetary field, it may happen in the industrial field as well. In England, the Industrial Revolution started in the north. Even by the early period of this century, most of the population and industrial trades were still concentrated in the northeast and northwest of England. Later, all concentrated in London. The same thing took place in Japan. The majority of Japan's pharmaceutical companies and other industrial groups came into being in Osaka. Now, many of them have established their headquarters in Tokyo. Although this trend is irreversible, the result will not necessarily be desirable. Perhaps, China should not follow this course, because it is too large and there are too many local dialects and cultural differences. Hence, it is better to have several stock exchanges at the initial stage; there is no need to strive to build a national unified stock exchange.

Some foreign experts do not support the idea of establishing too many trading halls in one country. They recommend the unified trading system developed by the Australians. In 1991, the trading halls of all six stock exchanges in Australia were closed and merged into a national unified market through establishing a "seat system." And this market is a completely automatic trading system through which all deals are concluded through brokerage. The advantage of the "seat system" is that it can satisfy the demands of customers from far away. The technology has caught the attention of other countries. Recently, it was adopted in Switzerland.

Section 2 Supervisory and Administrative System of China's Stock Trading Market

1. How to Improve the Supervisory and Administrative System of the Stock Trading Market.

The supervisory and administrative system of the stock market includes not only regulation of the primary market but also the secondary market. The regulation of the secondary market is further divided into many facets and levels, such as self-imposed regulation by the bill brokers and by quoted companies, the internal system of complaint, the regulation over securities agents by stock exchanges as autonomous organizations, as well as the regulation by the state over stock exchanges, securities trading networks and agents.

Since 1986 when China opened the secondary market for securities, securities dealing organizations have developed very quickly, now including nearly 100 specialized securities houses, several hundred trust and investment companies, comprehensive banks, as well as a large number of business departments which are independent legal persons and perform independent accounting. Altogether there are more than 1,000 securities establishments now. In view of the current situation, the supervisory and administrative system for the secondary market can be divided into two levels.

The first level is the subject of the regulation, that is, who performs the regulation. At the bottom level, it refers to the regulation enforced by the securities autonomous organizations over the securities agents, in addition to the self-imposed regulation by the securities agents.

The second level is the regulation by the state, that is, the regulation by government. At present, the regulation by government departments is like this: The People's Bank of China, as the major government department in charge of monetary organizations, is responsible for the examination and approval, establishment, termination, rescission as well as administration of securities establishments, while the China Securities Supervisory and Administrative Committee is responsible for the regulation of the routine business of the securities establishments. The formation of this pattern is directly related to the fact that during the 1986-88 period some major non-banking institutions handled securities transfer business. The Securities Supervisory and Administrative Committee has been in operation for a relatively short period of time, and it has not worked out a complete set of rules for the overall supervisory and administrative system.

Many experts hold that China should proceed from three aspects to study and improve its securities supervisory and administrative system.

First, the securities industry now practices a "free entry system." When established, all securities organizations were given rights to do business by the departments in charge of their examination and approval. In this way, be it a securities house or a trust and investment company, it would immediately have the right to handle securities, stocks in particular, once its establishment is approved. When the securities establishments were few and the business volume was small, the shortcomings of this system were not obvious. It even played a very important role for the development of the stock market then. But, along with further development of the stock market, the problem of regulation has become more and more outstanding. Further and normal development of the market in the future depends to a great extent on the upholding and stress of the principles of openness, fairness and equality in the market.

China is gradually moving toward establishing a license system. For those establishments which have been given the right to do securities business, their conditions should also be examined to see if they are up to the requirements for doing business in securities and to make the business proceed regularly. If they are not, a time limit can be imposed on them to meet the requirements or they must stop doing business in securities. The Shenzhen branch of the People's Bank of China has already begun to try out this system. It has issued licenses to those securities establishments and adopted the practice of annual checks. This is a useful experiment.

Second, how should the local regulation be made to dovetail and be compatible with national regulation? How should the separated local regulation be gradually developed into national unified regulation?

Since the stock exchanges in Shanghai and Shenzhen are the national centers for concentrated trading in securities, particularly shares, all regulation experiments have been made exclusively at these two exchanges. So far, these experiments both produced successes and showed shortcomings, that is, these two stock exchanges have somewhat different systems. In the future, the two stock exchanges will continue to be the national centers for concentrated trading.

At the same time, along with the development of the economy and the stock market, the possibility of setting up stock exchanges in other cities cannot be excluded. If a new stock exchange is established, what supervisory and administrative system should be adopted for it? Should it be supervised and managed according to a national unified system, or should national unified principles be worked out and the various places follow the principles should they establish different supervisory and administrative systems in accordance with their specific conditions? Priority should be given to studying these problems, which should be tackled after the China Securities Supervisory and Administrative Committee is able to perform its duties regularly.

Third, the regulation should be concentrated within the stock exchanges and the trading networks. One extremely important content of regulation is how to distinguish self-operated business by agents and trading on commission. The major aim of regulation is to ensure that the market is open, fair and equal; the specific task is to fight against cheating, insider trading as well as law, discipline and regulations violations. The area in which most troubles appear is the intermingling of self-operated business with trading on commission by agents. The development of the self-operated business is one very important condition for the stability of the market. Yet, for a period in the past, many complaints were lodged in this respect: Some securities agents who engage in both self trading and transactions on commission infringed upon the interests of investors who had commissioned them for their own interests. Therefore, this point should be a major part of China's future regulations over securities institutions: how to certify the securities agents who have the qualifications for self-operated business and how to separate the regulation over the securities agents in self-operated business from transactions on commission. With the solution of the above-mentioned three problems, it can be predicted that a fairly new type of supervisory and administrative system will take initial shape in China. Coupled with the autonomous regulation by the stock exchanges, the self-management regulation by the securities institutions as well as the regulation by state departments over the securities industry, a fairly comprehensive supervisory and administrative system which coordinates well both vertically and horizontally will eventually be formed.

In terms of the supervisory and administrative system for the stock market, the following problems call for urgent study and solution:

First, the system of supervision and control. To begin with, what departments have the right to regulate. For instance, it is said that the China Securities Supervisory and Administrative Committee, the People's Bank of China, the stock exchanges, the securities associations and the public rating organizations all have the right. But, what specific rights do they have? How should they share the work and coordinate with one another? And how should the question of mutual restraint between these departments be handled? Departments concerned should study these problems.

Moreover, should there be one level of supervisory and administrative organs, or more? The companies in China have been basically established according to administrative divisions. Of the securities houses, there are big as well as small ones, and there are ones that specialize in the securities industry as well as ones that do business in securities and other areas. Should they all be supervised and controlled by the China Securities Supervisory and Administrative Committee? Who should be responsible for deciding the setup and levels of the supervisory and administrative system? In other words, what system should the China Securities Supervisory and Administrative Committee adopt?

Second, at present China adopts the following forms of regulation: (a) Written management and financial reports submitted to supervisory departments at regular intervals; (b) supervisory personnel are sent to enterprises to make management and financial checkups; and (c) random inspections. Now, the forms of securities agent regulation are not very clear. The scope of business for securities houses needs to be studied. Judging by their current development, securities houses would be like trust companies or department stores, that is, they can engage in whatever lines of business they see fit. Theoretically speaking, the securities industry should be separated from banking. Yet, securities can absorb part of savings and invest it in industrial companies, such as real estate and trade companies. Regulation in these areas remain blanks.

Third, should regulation cover securities houses, stock exchanges, accounting firms, rating firms and securities associations? It is necessary to state clearly the regulation target, otherwise, it will cause a lot of trouble for the intermediary organizations.

Fourth, the contents of regulation by various departments should be clarified. For instance, the focus of financial regulation is rather clear: Primary attention is devoted to the enterprises' finances and tax payments. The aim is to see whether an enterprise has violated pertinent finance laws and regulations or whether it has dodged tax payments.

Some experts hold that it is imperative to pay close attention to relations between national administration and local administration. If the administration in various places is different, some people will take advantage of the loopholes. Hence, the administration of the stock market must follow unified rules.

Experts have also expressed their opinions on the role to be played by the China Securities Supervisory and Administrative Committee in improving China's stock market supervisory and administrative system. China's securities market is an immature market, and still younger — in its infancy — is the stock market. As the foundation of the stock market, China's joint-stock companies, particularly their reforms geared towards adopting the joint-stock system, are very much unconventional. Consequently, the stock market experiences greater fluctuations, and more investors make short-term speculations rather than long-term investments. The reason lies in the fact that China's securities industry legislation remains incomplete and the supervisory and administrative system is still less than adequate.

The Chinese government, however, has worked to lay the organizational foundation necessary to establish the supervisory and administrative system for the securities industry. The administrative organs, the State Council Securities Committee as well as the China Securities Supervisory and Administrative Committee, have been established. Since their establishment, the two committees have done a great deal of work, mainly in enacting laws and regulations regarding the securities industry. So far, more than a dozen laws and regulations have been promulgated in succession, including provisions on the administration of the open issue and trading of shares. The implementation of these laws and regulations will help the securities industry embark on a track of healthy development.

In the past, shares were openly issued only in Shanghai and Shenzhen. In 1993, the scope of the experiment of openly issuing shares was extended; every province, autonomous region and city which independently draws up a plan for economic development can now experiment in the open issue of shares. Therefore, it is an extremely urgent task to strengthen legislation and improve the supervisory and administrative system of the securities industry. It is necessary to establish not only a national supervisory and administrative system but also corresponding regional and local supervisory and administrative systems. It is very important not only to establish a government-enforced supervisory and administrative system but also intermediary organizations and an autonomous administrative system. The autonomous administration will be enforced by the stock exchanges, the securities associations as well as the numerous intermediary organizations.

The aim of the China Securities Supervisory and Administrative Committee should be to promote the healthy development of China's stock market rather than restrict its development, still less hinder it. It should create the conditions necessary for the healthy development of the stock market so as to make it develop more soundly and quickly.

2. International Experience in the Regulation of the Stock Trading Market.

The United States has established a multi-level supervisory and administrative system. Regulation at the upper-most level is enforced by the Securities and Exchange Commission (SEC), which enforces regulations not only covering the capital market but also the companies that raise funds on the capital market and monetary institutions.

The second level of regulation relies on the most important stock exchange markets, including the New York Stock Exchange, the National Association of Securities Dealers (NASD) and the local stock exchanges. Since the launching of NASDAQ, quoted companies have included not only American companies but also enterprises set up with overseas capital. Nevertheless, the rules for administration are basically identical. The most important securities management law is the Federal Stock Exchanges Act; next come the various stipulations adopted by different stock markets concerning quoted companies and listed shares. Therefore, no matter whether a company is quoted on the American Stock Exchange, on stock exchanges in the locality where it is located, at the New York Stock Exchange or on NASD, it must observe the unified rules for open and fair trading.

The third level of regulation covers control over brokerage organizations. The most important administrative authority for brokers is an autonomous organization — the National Association of Securities Dealers. The association has its headquarters in Washington and branch organizations throughout the country. Its major responsibility is to govern broker operations, ensuring normal and fair transactions. If any broker makes unfair deals, it will be automatically banned from the capital market. In order to prevent cheating, the securities legislation in the United States clearly states various kinds of fraudulent conduct as well as deals by insiders that are banned, and includes special stipulations regarding the activities of senior managerial personnel and major shareholders of listed companies. According to the stipulations, the top brass of quoted companies must make reports about all transactions in the companies' securities and return to the companies the profit derived from short-term trading activities. This means that if senior managers sell company shares they bought less than six months ago, they cannot retain any of the profit reaped by the sale; it must be returned to the company in full. In short, people who have insider knowledge about a company are absolutely not allowed to engage in short-term trading in that company's shares.

In the American legislation, stipulations banning unfair deals in securities cover a wide range, including those banning cheating activities in securities transactions, those banning the spreading of rumors and those banning insider trading.

Another important aspect of the regulation is the self-imposed restrictions by the brokers, including the supervision and control enforced by the stock market over various trading activities. In addition, it includes routine supervision by the government and checks by auditing institutions.

One important aspect in maintaining fair deals on the market and preventing insider deals is to ensure that listed companies disclose relevant financial and operational information to the public. With the establishment of an information disclosure system, there will be no opportunities for insider trading. All major stock exchanges in the United States demand that all quoted companies publicly disclose information about their major moves in line with the procedures for trading on the market.

Section 3 Fight Against Fraudulent Conduct in the Stock Trading Market

In order to maintain stock market order and protect the lawful rights and interests of investors and the interests of the public, legislation which prohibits fraudulent conduct in and promotes standardization of securities issuing and trading is necessary. This has become a significant problem, arousing widespread concern from Chinese society, particularly investors in securities.

1. Common Expressions of Fraudulent Conduct: Insider Trading, False Descriptions, Price Manipulation and Cheating Customers.

Fraudulent conduct refers to deceptive or spurious actions by units or individuals in the securities business that aim at reaping benefits and reducing losses.

First, insider trading refers to people who directly or indirectly take advantage of their inside knowledge in buying and selling securities to earn illegal economic benefits.

Second, false or misleading descriptions refer to giving false, unreal or misleading explanations about the nature, prospects and legal connotations concerning the issuing and trading of securities, or withholding key information in giving explanations to clients or other people. These actions then lead clients to make wrong investment decisions and reap economic benefits for the trader or investment concern involved in the deal.

Third, price manipulation refers to wilfully making use of information, the fund under one's management, one's administrative power or one's personal influence to produce false situations on the market which induce investors to make misguided investment decisions. This, with the aim of reaping illegal economic benefits for oneself or the company one works for.

Fourth, directly cheating customers refers to making use of one's position as consignor, custodian or agent to make securities deals that harm the interests of investors, or other consignors, custodians and agents, thus reaping illegal economic benefits for themselves in the process.

2. Fraudulent Conduct on China's Stock Market and Countermeasures Needed.

China's stock market has experienced the fraudulent conduct described above. Moreover, it has also been haunted by problems that underdeveloped stock markets everywhere go through at the beginning stages of development.

First, generally speaking, the development of China's stock market has been sound. Control over internal shares has been strengthened and proper governmental guidarce has been given. But, other steps still need to be taken to prevent units and people from taking advantage of stock market for personal gains. Recently, domestic investors in China have been very anxious to invest in the stock market. This scenario was typical: enterprises and units would take the liberty of issuing internal shares, part of which were also issued simultaneously to the public, without obtaining the approval of the appropriate departments in charge. They set the issue price at the nominal value or with a certain premium, normally one or two times the nominal value. They not only issued shares at relatively low price but also, to goad people to buy them, made statements suggesting that their shares would be listed on the stock exchange later in that year, or the next year, or a certain year in the future. At the same time, they manipulated off-the-book transactions (with or without intention) and unloaded the shares in their hands when the price on the black market rose to a certain level, earning a large amount of money as a result. Whether the shares in question could be listed and traded at the time they declared, they themselves did not know. Although the Chinese government had stipulated that internal shares were not allowed to be traded for a period of three years, and the news media had reported this information, some investors remained ignorant of it, or they had bought the shares on the secondary or circulation market at high prices before they learned of the stipulations. This situation has become a fairly difficult problem to tackle.

Second, some necessary laws and regulations regarding the stock market have not yet been enacted, some existing laws call for amendment and some trading operation systems lack necessary hardware. Some people have taken advantage of these loopholes, resulting in unequal competition. Take the problem of mutual funds (investment trusts) for example. Some places have established them while other places wanted to establish them but did not have the proper conditions in place yet; some places have put them into the market but failed to manage them effectively; while other places have used them on the black market. Because the market is not unified, it is impossible to form reasonable competitive prices.

The following are major problems that have plagued China's fledgling stock market:

(a) Dealers at some securities institutions have made use of their position to obtain favors for their relatives and friends. Since there are intervals from the time when they receive commissions from customers to the time when the orders are keyed into the stock exchange's automatic matching system, they used these time lapses to place orders for their relatives and friends first, disregarding the proper sequence or orders placed and prices offered.

(b) Some members of the news media have deliberately made

false comments to mislead people or cause price fluctuations on the stock market with the purpose to disposing of their shares. And, more seriously, in exchange for bribes some journalists published articles with untrue statements which favored certain quoted companies.

(c) Some securities institutions and dealers even turned the shares customers put in their custody into collateral, using them in their purchases and sales of securities.

(d) Some securities institutions violated China's regulations regarding the stock market to engage in a massive margin business, collecting unlawful interest which ended up lining private purses.

(e) Some units and some major share buyers collaborated very closely, despite the absence of written agreements, to pool funds to manipulate the price of certain shares.

(f) Some people used their insider information to give direct or indirect suggestions to others in buying or selling certain shares, causing a sudden rise or fall in prices one day before the dividend distribution announcement was made.

Then, what measures should be adopted to fight fraudulent conduct on China's stock market and effectively protect the interests of the investors?

First, it is necessary to study and promote the enactment of various laws and regulations to ensure the sound development of the stock market, including regulations regarding the issuing and trading of securities and regulations regarding the management of stock exchanges and securities institutions, particularly regulations regarding the prevention of fraudulent conduct in securities, so as to bring into play the supervisory role of the China Securities Supervisory and Administrative Committee according to law.

Second, it is necessary to give full play to the autonomous role of securities associations, strengthen the autonomy of the securities industry and stock exchanges, and reinforce the functions of the board of supervisors.

Third, the China Securities Supervisory and Administrative Committee should be given access to the computer operation systems of the two stock exchanges so they can obtain first-hand knowledge of every securities deal.

Fourth, despite its limited manpower and financial resources now, the China Securities Supervisory and Administrative Committee should nevertheless learn from other countries about enforcing securities industry regulations and laws. In particular, they should work hard to develop supervisory software systems, establish computer automated warning systems, collect timely information about law violations in securities trading and strengthen supervision and administration over the stock market in conjunction with other means and instruments.

Section 4 The Administration of Stock Market Intermediary Organizations

1. Regular Administration of Stock Market Intermediary Organizations Should Be Developed Simultaneously with the Stock Market.

Although China's stock market has been late in starting, its scale has continuously expanded and developed, giving rise to some new features in recent years. (a) The primary market has developed rapidly, with the number of quoted companies and the amount of shares supplied rising markedly. The listing of shares issued by state-owned large and medium-sized enterprises, in particular, has played a very important role in the development of the stock market. The scope of experimentation regarding quoted companies has gradually extended from Shanghai and Shenzhen to all parts of the country. (b) The secondary market has constantly expanded, with stock trading gradually radiating from Shanghai and Shenzhen to other large and medium-sized cities throughout the country. Members of the two stock exchanges elsewhere that have computer terminals linked with the Shanghai and Shenzhen stock exchanges have multiplied. (c) Investors have matured. Having experienced the vicissitudes of the stock market over the past few years, they have acquired a stronger sense of risks and can better stand market changes. (d)

Legislation has gradually improved and a supervisory and administrative system that guides the issuing and trading of shares has been established.

During the course of development, intermediary organizations, such as securities houses, accounting firms, law firms as well as the asset appraisal companies, have shouldered the task of linking issuers with investors, and sellers with buyers on the primary and secondary markets. They have undergone a course of simultaneous development and growth with the stock market itself. The development of the stock market calls for these intermediary organizations to play the role of economic police, that is, enfocing strict examinations and checkups, ratings and other related supervisory work over enterprises that publicly issue shares. At the same time they should take corresponding legal responsibilities for the authenticity and integrity of relevant materials publicly issued and circulated by these enterprises, so as to ensure that trading in securities is open, fair and equal. Therefore, the establishment and standardization of these intermediary organizations directly affects the fairness and effectiveness of the stock market and has a direct bearing on investor interests, and hence is of paramount importance.

2. Intermediary Organizations Lack Independence and Professional Personnel, Are Unable to Perform Their Duties Adequately and Violations of Pertinent Laws and Provisions Have Occurred Now and Then.

Here are the major problems that have occured in the development of China's securities intermediary organizations.

(1) The intermediary organizations lack independence in operation.

Theoretically speaking, intermediary organizations should operate and bear legal responsibilities independently and subject to supervision by the government and the public. In fact, however, this is precisely what China has failed to achieve. The major reasons are: (a) China's stock market has only been under development for a short time and pertinent laws and provisions regarding securities are still being enacted; also, the supervisory and administrative system is still being formed. (b) The intermediary organizations themselves lack experience and the necessary technological means, and their development is uneven. (c) As any problem arising in the issue and trading of securities is sensitive and the influence of the planned economic system still exerts itself, the government has to resort to administrative means. Moreover, as China's system for stock market administration has not yet been well established, there is still the lack of cooperation between different governmental departments.

Due to these reasons, it is hard for China's securities houses, accounting firms, law firms and property assessment companies to operate and shoulder legal responsibilities independently. On the other hand, governmental departments (such as the authorities in charge, finance and taxation departments) are excessively involved in the specific work of the structural reform as well as the technical and commercial activities related to the issue and trading of securities, which makes it impossible for them to concentrate on enacting new laws and enforcing the existing ones, and investigate and prosecute violations of the laws.

(2) The intermediary organizations have not been able to perform their duties adequately.

Over the past few years, a large number of national and local securities organizations have been established. Added to those set up formerly, they have formed a network of considerable scale. Yet, few among them can offer package and specialized services in securities underwriting and marketing, brokerage, property management and investment consultation.

The same problem exists in the development of other intermediary organizations. As they have only come to the stock market for a very short period of time and lack the necessary professional expertise and an accepted code of conduct, it is hard for them to play their supervisory role effectively.

Under the precondition that the legal and administrative systems for the stock market still left much to be desired, some intermediary organizations have overlooked their self-improvement, replaced sound professional services with administrative interference from the government and background relations, and engaged in unfair competition. Such act has adversely affected the fairness, effectiveness and standardization of the stock market.

(3) Violations by intermediary organizations against pertinent laws and regulations have frequently occurred.

The intermediary organizations and their employees should follow the principle of "being diligent and responsible" in work. To be more specific, intermediary organizations should, while performing their duties, observe the standard professional and moral codes required of the securities industry. They should make reasonable efforts to check and validate written or oral reports submitted to government departments as well as notices, prospectuses for stock subscription and professional suggestions directed towards the public. In practice, however, violations of this principle and even offences against the law and pertinent regulations have occurred from time to time, as manifested in fraudulent practices in the issue of securities, the supply of false and unreasonable documents as well as legal documents that contain misleading contents or have important omissions, violating the regulations to accept commissions in securities deals, ganging up in self-operated securities operations and engaging in margin trading.

Such misdeeds fall into two categories: One occurs because the intermediary organizations themselves lack the necessary professional expertise and practical experience; the other happens because they desire to be the winners in the fierce market competition and therefore wilfully commit offences against the law and pertinent regulations. Of course, their emergence is related to the fact that China's legal system has not been well established yet and the penalties meted out are far too lenient and lack the coercive strength, and that the administrative system for the stock market has not been well established. In any case, the occurrence of such phenomena has adversely affected the sound development of China's stock market.

(4) Intermediary organizations lack well-trained professional workers.

In a mature stock market, people are the key if securities houses, accounting firms, law firms, property assessment companies and other intermediary organizations wish to compete and survive in the marketplace and play their due role as economic police. China's intermediary organizations are now in urgent need of a contingent of well-educated, hard-working, responsible professionals who are well versed in knowledge about securities and international conventions regarding the securities business. This is the current situation in China and a problem inherent in all fledgling stock markets in developing countries.

3. In the Establishment and Management of Intermediary Organizations, It Is Necessary for China to Strengthen Its Legal System, Enforce Checks on the Organizations' Qualifications, Learn from the Experience of Other Countries, Train Personnel and Enforce Scientific Regulation.

Monetary experts have advanced the following major proposals to strengthen stock market intermediary organizations:

(1) Strengthening efforts to establish an effective legal system regarding the securities industry so as to make it possible for departments that supervise intermediary organizations to follow set legal stipulations.

As an important part of the socialist market economy, China's stock market must operate according to the norms of law. The lack of effective legal means for the administration over the stock market (including intermediary organizations) has become a major obstacle hindering further sound development of China's stock market. At present, the conditions for enacting such laws have ripened: Valuable experience has been gained over the past few years regarding the running of the stock market; Shanghai and Shenzhen have enacted local laws and regulations; and the State Commission for Restructuring the Economy and other departments have put forward a series of proposals to standardize the experiment in the joint-stock system. Therefore, it is necessary to accelerate the pace of legislative work and make sure the laws and regulations to be enacted coordinate with and complement one another.

In enacting laws and regulations for the securities industry, China should learn from international conventions and, proceeding from China's realities, establish a legal framework as described below: Taking the *Law on Securities* as the basic law for the stock market, and taking the *Stock Trading Law, Investment Bank Law, Law Governing Stock Houses, Law Governing Investment Companies, Law Regarding Management of Funds, Corporation Law, Accountants Law*, and *Lawyers Law* as major parts of the framework; these laws should be fitted well with the *Code of Conduct for Employers in the Securities Industry, Provisions for Protecting Investors* and *Provisions for Giving Penalties to Transactions by Insiders*. This will enable the stock market to remain open, fair, highly efficient and unified and make it possible to protect the legitimate rights and interests of investors.

To improve this legal system, it is also necessary to establish law-enforcing organizations which can help foster the development of the stock market through enforcing relevant laws and regulations. These law-enforcing organizations include government supervisory and administrative departments, securities supervisory and administrative committees, stock exchanges, securities dealers' associations, accountants' associations, lawyers' associations and property-assessment associations.

(2) Intensifying qualification checks over intermediary organizations.

China has made satisfactory progress in checking the qualifications of intermediary organizations. The Ministry of Finance and the China Securities Supervisory and Administrative Committee jointly decreed the *Provisions for Affirming the Qualifications of Accounting Firms and Registered Accountants Involved in the Securities Industry*, and a number of accounting firms have had their qualifications affirmed. The Ministry of Justice and the China Securities Supervisory and Administrative Committee co-signed and promulgated the *Provisional Regulations on Affirming the Qualifications of Lawyers and Law Firms Involved in Securities Industry*.

Examining and affirming the qualifications of intermediary

organizations and people engaged in securities industry is a long-term, never-ending job. In line with the development of China's stock market, strict requirements should be formulated for work credentials and fair competition should also be introduced. People and organizations that are qualified should be issued licenses and credentials so as to ensure the professional standards of the intermediary organizations and their employees. Qualified intermediary organizations and their employees can draw from a reserve fund for professional liability risks and write professional liability insurance policies. Moreover, both severe punishment and the mechanism of interest which is characterized by high salaries should be used to encourage the employees in the securities industry to abide by law conscientiously and foster among them a sound sense of responsibility and hard work.

(3) Strengthening supervision over intermediary organizations.

The control and supervision over intermediary organizations are an important part of the regulation of the securities market. Take Hong Kong for example. After the stock market crisis in 1987, it reorganized its securities industry administrative framework. In the new administrative system, the securities and futures supervisory committee is made the highest organ of power, while the Hong Kong Stock Exchange is given the major responsibility for routine supervisory work; commercial banks, accounting and law firms shall follow the codes of conduct in their respective fields. The supervisory work at the above three levels reinforces and supplements each other.

China's securities supervisory and administrative system is now being established. Yet, there is still a long way to go for it to develop into a well-established system in which the supervisory and administrative organizations at different levels not only perform their own duties but also seek coordination with one another. It is particularly so with regard to the self-disciplinary administration by intermediary organizations, because the horizontally framed associations, which serve as their autonomous organizations, are still being in the process of being established. In this respect, China can follow the example of the United

States. In the U.S., the National Association of Securities Dealers enforces the regulation over the securities dealers. The power of NASD covers a wide range, including the rating of the securities dealers, the examination and affirmation of the qualifications of people employed in the securities industry, as well as the enactment of self-disciplinary provisions. These provisions demand the securities dealers to abide by the law and enforce self-discipline among themselves. When violations against pertinent law and regulations occur, the association can first give moral condemnations and then, if warranted, administer legal punishment.

In forming the securities supervisory and administrative system, another important issue is to make clear distinctions between the supervisory and administrative functions and roles of the government and that of the autonomous organizations. In addition, the de facto situation that "banking is not separated from the securities industry" must be handled correctly. Government administration over the market should be detached from routine affairs and be somewhat elastic, and banking should be divorced from the securities industry — these are two important prerequisites. Only in this way can the regulation over the securities market be well-knit and yet not lose elasticity.

(4) Attaching importance to the training of professionals.

To develop China's own securities intermediary organizations, it is imperative to rely on the country's own contingent of securities professionals. The task of training professionals in the securities business should be jointly shouldered by the intermediary organizations, the various associations of the intermediary organizations, as well as government supervisory departments. The methods used to improve professional expertise can include: conducting on-the-job training, giving time off from work to take classes, and sending people abroad for intensive training.

(5) Learn from the advanced technology and managerial expertise of foreign intermediary organizations.

Along with the further development of China's stock market, more and more domestic enterprises will issue foreign exchange shares or directly list their shares in overseas stock exchanges. Consequently, more and more famous foreign intermediary organizations will be involved in the work, (some specialized organizations overseas in fact have already been involved: subscribing shares issued by Chinese enterprises, providing legal consultation, etc.) No doubt, all this will provide the opportunity for China to learn from their advanced technology and managerial expertise.

In order to promote the growth of domestic intermediary organizations, some Sino-foreign cooperative or joint-venture intermediary organizations can be established. So far, several joint-venture firms in accounting have been set up in China and they have been involved in the accounting and auditing of domestic enterprises which issue shares overseas. When the conditions are ripe, it is highly possible to establish Sino-foreign joint-venture securities houses or to set up domestic securities branches in other countries, so as to promote the standardization and internationalization of Chinese intermediary stock organizations.

Chapter 4
The Circulation of Public Equity

Section 1 Necessities and Difficulties in the Circulation of Public Equity

1. The Circulation of Public Equity Is Conducive for Optimizing Resource Distribution, the Appreciation of Assets and the Stability of the Stock Market.

It will not do that public equity is not allowed to circulate. The same variety of shares issued by the same enterprise should enjoy the same rights. This is a basic principle of a shareholding economy. But on China's stock market the implementation of this principle has been seriously hampered, as manifested in the following: The common A shares (private) are allowed to be traded on the Shanghai and Shenzhen stock exchanges, while only a small amount of corporate equity is allowed to be traded. State equity is not allowed to be traded at all. In recent years, the Chinese stock market has experienced big ups and downs. People have been eager to speculate in shares while not so enthusiastic about keeping them. Consequently, it has been difficult to improve the stock market mechanism. All this is directly related to the fact that the public equity is not allowed to be traded on the market.

It is the goal of China's economic reform to establish the socialist market economic system. As an important component of modern market economy, the stock market also plays important roles in promoting the maturity of China's market economy. However, if publicly owned shares are not allowed to be circulated in the market, the stock market cannot develop properly and its multiple functions will not be brought into full play.

Public equity should be allowed to be listed and traded because:

First, it stresses equality and free transactions on the stock market. Through the buying and selling of shares, it is possible that shares formerly held by government departments and legal persons find their way into the hands of individual citizens, while shares originally held by the latter can also be transferred to the former. On the one hand, this represents a breakthrough in the barriers imposed by the ownership relations between the various sectors of the traditional economy; it makes it possible for resources to circulate and be effectively distributed within the whole society and frees enterprises from the yokes of ownership to enter the market and subject themselves to the supervision and restraints of society. On the other hand, citizens will, persuant to their own interests, devote more attention to the operation and achievements of the enterprises, thus improving their qualities as investors.

Since public equity is not allowed to be circulated on the market, it ensures that the publicly owned sector is able to maintain a majority share in quoted companies: On the one hand, it enables government departments to, by means of their holding positions, continue to exercise control over the quoted companies and operate with no distinction between governemnt administration and enterprise management. On the other hand, it makes the individual shareholders feel that they have little say in the quoted companies. In fighting to maintain its holding position, the publicly owned capital inevitably becomes stagnant: resources are not circulated and redistributed according to natural market forces. Therefore, individual investors, in order to safeguard their own interests, turn their attention away from the enterprises and focus on the stock market — that is, to reap gains for themselves and express their common wishes through the fluctuations of stock price. In a certain sense, it can be said that the inequality between public equity and personal shares on the stock market is related to the inequality of their stock rights in enterprises and their different positions in ownership relations. Nevertheless, these inequalities cause unnatural movement in the stock market and are opposed by the market economy.

Second, one important function of the stock market is to adjust the distribution of resources between the various industrial sectors and enterprises: On the one hand, resources are better concentrated in industries and enterprises that hold promising prospects for development and profits. This helps optimize the industrial mix and develop enterprises. On the other hand, it makes resources flow out of "sunset" industries and backward enterprises, eventually eliminating unprofitable ones. In the whole process, the stock market constantly evaluates industries and enterprises through price fluctuations. These evaluations are actually evaluations by society. If public equity is allowed to be traded on the market, the evaluation by society is jointly performed by the government departments (state equity), the various legal person organizations (corporate equity) and the citizens (private shares), and thus is strongly objective and compulsory. The situation is vastly different if public equity is not allowed to circulate. When public equity is not freely traded it gives people a signal: Government departments and the legal person organizations, to safeguard their own interest, will not turn a blind eye towards the operation of the quoted companies, and enterprises will not be eliminated no matter what. Therefore, people can rest assured and place their demands of the quoted companies on the holders of the public equity and engage wantonly in speculation on stocks. This signal exerted a strong influence on people's psyche in 1990 when stock prices at the Shenzhen Stock Exchange skyrocketed. This was also true in 1992 when stock prices at the Shanghai Stock Exchange rose astronautically. In these situations, the price fluctuations of shares issued by quoted companies can neither reflect a true evaluation by society nor by the holders of private shares. Consequently, the function of the stock market to promote industrial mix optimization and enterprise development is also greatly weakened.

At present, in shareholding enterprises public equity accounts for 90 percent and private shares account for only 10 percent. Of all public equity, the shares owned by the state are converted from the original assets and hence represent the remaining value of the assets, while the corporate equity represents the increased value of the assets. If all public equity, that is, both the remaining value and increased value of the original assets, are not allowed to circulate, while only the private shares are allowed, it will be impossible to realize the goal of optimizing the distribution of resources through the stock market.

Third, the circulation of public equity is conducive to the appreciation of corporate equity.

Some people worry that the circulation of corporate equity on the market might affect the dominant position of the publicly owned economic sector. This is not the case because the often-said dominant position of the publicly owned economic sector refers to the situation in the country as a whole rather than in a particular enterprise. It is insignificant whether the publicly owned economic sector holds the dominant position in a particular enterprise or department. Conversely, not allowing corporate equity to circulate will result in a reduction of the ratio of the public equity in the stock rights structure of the enterprises. This is because the personal equity ratio in a company's stock makeup can increase as a result of increased investment, but corporate equity does not enjoy this advantage. The share of public equity does not have the fund for increased investment, and consequently the ratio of public equity in the total will decrease. If corporate equity is allowed to circulate, its ratio in the equity makeup not only can be maintained but also be increased through possible appreciation of its value.

Fourth, the circulation of public equity is required if enterprises are to change their management mechanism.

An important goal to establish the shareholding system is to separate government administration from enterprise management and ensure that enterprises enjoy independence in production and management. But, the current way of managing state equity makes it hard to realize this goal. Theoretically speaking, the highest power organ of a shareholding company is the conference of shareholders, and the representatives of the holders of state equity can use their rights at the conference to influence the company's important policy decisions. Provided the decisions adopted at the conference of shareholders do not transgress the economic policies and law of the state, government departments should not interfere. Yet, in practice, questions concerning the basic rights of the shareholding companies cannot be solved by the conference of shareholders; even if resolutions are adopted at the conference of shareholders on some questions, they still have to be submitted to government departments for examination and approval. This inevitably results in a situation in which government administration and enterprise management are not separated: there is too much administrative interference and the conduct of the enterprises is not standardized.

For instance, when a shareholding company decides to increase its issuance of shares and intends to sell each share at a certain price (say, at the market price), this will force the state to increase its investment in the company by millions and even billions of yuan if the state equity is also to be increased. In such a situation, the state, on the one hand, obviously does not have sufficient economic resources to respond to the company's plan to increase its stock, and on the other, no representative of state equity has the right to make decisions over such matters. The inevitable result is that the department in charge of the company, the financial department and the department responsible for the management of state property will one after another interfere with the decision of the enterprise, giving rise to a situation in which the government administrative departments and the shareholding company plunge into endless haggling over a series of questions, such as the amount of new shares to be issued and the distribution of dividends. Yet, this situation of too much administrative interference and integration between government administration and enterprise management obviously runs counter to the initial aim of the reform to establish the shareholding system.

Fifth, only when public equity is freely circulated can it maintain its ratio in the stock makeup.

The purpose of not allowing public equity to circulate is to maintain the ratio held by public equity in enterprises' stock makeups. Yet, it is impossible to maintain the ratio unchanged. On the one hand, the value of public equity cannot be increased if it does not circulate. Therefore, publicly owned enterprises and units will be unwilling to invest in public equity and so the amount of public equity will not increase. On the other hand, the quoted companies, in order to increase their capital, can distribute new shares to old shareholders (in a ratio equal to the amount of shares they originally held) at prices lower than the market price and higher than the nominal value. Of course, foreign and domestic individual shareholders will be very enthusiastic about the increased issue of shares. As a result, after every new issue, foreign investment shares and private shares will increase, while the ratio of public equity will come down because no new investment is made.

Take the quoted companies in Shenzhen for example. The ratio of state equity in all the companies has come down after several expanded issues: In the Development Bank, the ratio of state equity came down from 25.18 percent at the time when the shares were first listed to 19.76 percent in the first half of 1992; in Jintian Company, from 20.56 percent to 8.88 percent; in Wanke, from 19.2 percent to 17 percent; and in Anda Company, from 60 percent to 51.58 percent. Obviously, not allowing public equity to circulate cannot maintain their ratio in the stock makeup.

Sixth, the circulation of public equity is conducive to the stability of the stock market.

At present, public equities hold some rather large ratios in quoted companies. This is particularly so in large and medium-sized enterprises. For instance, of all the quoted companies in Shanghai, public equities account for about 93 percent. If public equity is allowed to be traded on the market, the scope of the market will be vastly expanded. This not only can alleviate the contradiction between supply and demand but also makes it hard for major individual shareholders to manipulate the market. Moreover, at certain periods public equity can play a market-regulating role. Therefore, not allowing public equity to circulate is unadvantageous to the stability and development of the stock market.

2. Obstacles for Public Equity to Enter the Market: Contradictions in Property Rights, Policy Limitations and Differences in Aims.

In China, public property has long operated within the framework of the traditional economy and been imprinted with its principles and mechanism. Although great changes have taken place in enterprises' operating mechanism and principles and publicly owned property has taken the forms of corporate and state equity in the process of introducing the shareholding system, the inherent mechanism of the publicly owned property has not witnessed much change. Thus, it is hard to coordinate the performance of public equity with the requirements of the stock market.

The obstacles for public equity to enter the market are as follows.

First, regarding contradictions in property rights, the stock market has two basic requirements: (1) those who come to the stock market must make investments with their own property and enjoy full initiative in the operation of the capital; (2) those who come to the market must bear all consequences resulting from their transactions in shares, that is, both enjoy benefits and bear losses. But, these two requirements cannot be fulfilled in the operation of public equity. Take state equity for example. First, the ownership of state equity property rights is not clear. In terms of direct relations, state equity is owned by government departments, and the subject of the property right is clear. But, if one considers it in detail, the owner of the property is not so clear: Government departments at which level own them? Take an enterprise at the city level for example. Which government at which level owns it? Is it the city government, or the provincial government, or the State Council? Is it owned by the government department in charge of the industry, or the financial department, or the department in charge of state-owned assets? No one can give a clear explanation. When the owner of the property right is not clear, it will be hard to be clear who has the right to operate the state equity. Second, it is not clear who should enjoy the rich returns and profits and how should they be shared when the state equity operates successfully. Nevertheless, when the state equity operates unsuccessfully and cause losses in capital, the operators must not only take responsibility for economic losses but also take political responsibility. When the interests and responsibilities are not on a reciprocal basis — great responsibilities and little benefits, no one dares to take a lighthearted action with regard to the listing of state equity in the stock market.

Second, policy limitations are also an obstacle for public equity circulation. For those who come to the stock market to deal in shares, selling means to give up their equity and retrieve capital, and buying means to acquire equity and make capital input. To regulate the direction of capital flow and the structure of capital is in every sense a normal act in the operation of capital. Yet, some policy-makers are used to viewing the equity structure from the angle of the ownership relations in the traditional economy. They think that, after state-owned enterprises are transformed into shareholding enterprises, state equity and corporate equity should occupy a holding position in every enterprise. And when public equity is traded in the stock market, the ratio of public equity in the enterprise's equity structure might fall, and this would indicate a change in the public nature of the enterprise. Therefore, they adopt policies that corporate equity can be traded only between legal persons and state equity is not allowed to be traded in the stock market.

Third, differences in aims hinder public equity circulation. To benefit from trading in shares is the basic aim of all people coming to the stock market. Therefore, it is natural that they make full use of all opportunities provided by price hikes and falls in the stock market to this end. But, with public equity, particularly state equity, the situation is different. For state-owned assets, there is the contradiction between reaping profits — an inherent requirement — and the responsibility to maintain the normal order of social life. Or, to put it another way, the contradiction between the requirements for capital and government responsibilities which, after the introduction of the shareholding system, has fallen onto state equity. In respect to the requirements for capital, in a situation when the prices on the stock market skyrocket, as appeared over the last few years, selling out state equity would make the capital represented by it increase by several or even several dozen fold; purchasing shares when prices on the stock market decline would greatly boost state equity. Therefore, it will be very profitable to operate state equity by taking advantage of fluctuations on the stock market.

Viewed from the angle of the government responsibilities, however, by coming to the market, state equity will probably manipulate the market with its great breadth of holdings — this not only is harmful to the stability and growth of the stock market itself, but also possible to produce a hidden danger in the stability of social life. When state equity is held in the hands of the government, a greater priority will be placed on the government responsibilities than the requirements for capital. Under such a situation, it should be taken for granted that state equity is not allowed to be traded on the stock market.

The concrete manifestations of the difficulty to coordinate well the operational mechanism of public equity and the requirements of the stock market can also be described in other ways. But, it is sufficient to see from the description above that the fundamental reason why it is hard for public equity to be listed and traded on the stock market lies in the disharmony between the principles and mechanism of the traditional economy implemented in the operation of public equity and the principles and mechanism of the market economy implemented on the stock market. Therefore, to allow public equity to enter the stock market, it is imperative to reform the principles and mechanism for the operation of public equity in line with the demands of the market economy.

To tackle the problem of the circulation of public equity, one point should first be clarified: how to understand the dominant position held by public ownership in shareholding enterprises and how to attain the goal. Saying that public ownership holds a dominant position, has three possible meanings: (1) That public ownership holds a dominant position in the total economy; (2) that in some important enterprises that have a direct bearing on the national economy and people's livelihood, public ownership holds a considerable ratio, say 40-60 percent; and (3) that in ordinary enterprises (not all), the ratio of public ownership only needs to reach a certain level to occupy a controlling position. And this might vary in line with the specific distribution of the equity rights: the more scattered the equity rights, the smaller the ratio of public ownership needs to be to hold a controlling position in an enterprise.

In line with these principles, when public equity in a given enterprise is sold, the money received can be invested in other enterprises. In this case, the amount of public equity is not reduced, and may even see some increase, because the capital held by public equity may have increased via selling and buying. Within a certain enterprise, when, after selling and buying, the ratio held by public equity has fallen below the level that should be maintained to keep a controlling position, legal persons and state holding companies can buy the necessary amount of shares to re-establish the desired public equity ratio. This ratio should be maintained via a dynamic state of buying and selling. It does not mean that it must be maintained all the time and under all conditions.

Another problem to be solved to enable public equity to be listed and traded on the market is: Who is entitled to manage public equity? Regarding public equity, corporate equity can be managed by enterprises' legal persons. Then, who should manage state equity? Would it be prudent to establish state equity holding companies who are empowered to manage the state equity? In line with the increase in shareholding companies, there should be a number of such companies. And among the holding companies, there should be competition. Monopoly should not be allowed. Experiments in establishing investment companies or holding companies are now carried out in Shenzhen and Xiamen.

Japan sells state equity in some enterprises and invested the new funds in other important economic sectors, so if China chooses to sell state equity, it will not be the first to do so. In line with the situation of different enterprises, China can adopt the practice of holding a certain ratio of shares and selling the remaining part. In selling part of its state equity, China will be able to enjoy the added benefit of absorbing new foreign investment. At present, there are approximately US$1.5 billion of capital in countries and regions around China seeking new grounds for investment.

3. To Successfully Bring Public Equity to the Market, It Is Necessary to Stipulate in Law that the Same Varieties of Shares Enjoy the Same Rights and Benefits, and that Holders of State Equity Have Decision-Making Power in Buying and Selling Shares.

Bringing public equity to the market is conducive to maintaining its dominant position. Yet, to ensure success in bringing it to the market, it is also necessary to solve two problems of principle.

First, it is necessary to stipulate in law that the same categories of shares must enjoy the same rights and benefits, all subjects of investments are equally footed and there should be no discrimination against anyone. This is because one of the basic principles of the stock market is to ensure competition on an equal footing. The prerequisite for competition on an equal footing is that all people who come to the market to trade should have equal access: no singular protection whatsoever should be given to any category of shares. Otherwise, it would be impossible for competition on an equal footing between those which are protected and those which are not.

If no special protection is given to public equity, then how can it be ensured that state-owned assets do not suffer any harm? In securities transactions, so long as the open, fair and equal principles are held and the various stipulations concerning securities trade are carried out, the interests of any party will not be infringed upon. If infringement occurs against the interests of any party, it should be dealt with according to law; there is no need to give special protection to a particular variety of shares. If a stipulation is made that no harm can befall state-owned assets, does this mean that the property of individuals can be infringed upon? There are bound to be profits and losses in the transactions of securities. If it is stipulated that the interests of state equity can incur no harm, that is, their value must be maintained or increased, does it mean that only individual shares are allowed to lose but not to win? Of course, it is a stipulation of the Chinese Constitution to protect the socialist publicly owned property, but it is also a stipulation of the Constitution to protect the legitimate property of citizens. Therefore, it would be better to give equal positions to different investment holders and let the same variety of shares enjoy the same rights.

Since no special protection should be given to public equity, it is then unnecessary to establish a separate market for trading public equity, because to set up a separate market is also a sort of protection, which is not advantageous to the state, either. (1) It is advantageous to pooling funds from society, because the current reality in China is that a large amount of excess funds are scattered in the hands of the people, while large numbers of state-owned large and medium-sized enterprises rely on state subsidies to keep going. This, coupled with the backwardness in the establishment of mutual funds (unit trusts), means that to establish a separate market for trading of state equity is tantamount to allowing only a few successfully managed enterprises to trade shares among themselves, while large numbers of state-owned enterprises stand aside watching. This results in private capital being excluded from the market. Moreover, the trading in shares must have gains and losses, and this includes state-owned enterprises. (2) The segmentation of the market, that is, the different markets for A and B shares and for public equity and private shares, inevitably leads to confusion. This is because different markets will naturally have different prices and have different ways of carrying out the principle of openness. Eventually, people who wish to make exorbitant profits will take advantage of the price gaps between these markets. In fact, the holders of state equity and private shareholders can buy from and sell to each other in a unified stock market; it is not necessary to set up independent markets for each. In addition, in the unified market, the holders of state equity can trade between themselves, and the state can take the opportunity to absorb private funds. This will be more advantageous to the country's economic development. But, as the state equity is in large amounts, proper arrangements must be made when they go into the market so that they will not cause a great shock to the stock market. (3) If a separate market is set up for state equity, the original stock market will still circulate private shares. In this situation, the problems mentioned previously, such as the contradiction between supply and demand, market manipulation, sharp price rises and falls, will remain. And the state still has not the strength to solve them. This is tantamount not only to "attending to one thing but losing sight of the other" but also to "falling between two stools." (4) In the unified market, state equity, corporate equity, private shares and foreign capital shares compete with one another. In the competition, state equity and corporate equity will undergo tests, enabling them to withstand fiercer storms in the future. To erect a protective shelter will not give them this benefit.

Second, it is necessary to stipulate that the holders of public equity have, in principle, decision-making power over the buying or selling of shares. The holders of public equity should be holding companies set up with the approval of the administrative department in charge of state-owned assets. The holding companies should have the right to make decisions over the disposal of shares they hold, and they do not have to apply for approval. The wording "in principle" means to treat some industries as exceptions, like transport and communications, energy, and telecommunications, all of which have been given priority in development. In these industries, if the selling of state equity will reduce the ratio held by the state below a predefined limit, applications must be made to authorities in charge for approval.

There are two reasons to allow the holders of public equity autonomy in making share transaction decisions. First, the shareholding system will not be implemented in projects that have a bearing on the country's security, involve sophisticated national defense technology or mining projects which are of strategic importance, and industries which are designated by the state as development priorities. The remaining are relatively unimportant, because their development will neither effect a change in the nature of society nor affect the fate of the state. Therefore, it is unnecessary to set a bottom limit for the ratio of shares to be held by the state in these industries. Since there should not be a bottom limit, it should be taken for granted that the holders of public equity have the right to make their own decisions regarding the buying and selling of shares they hold. Second, to respond to the quick changes that take place in the stock market, the holders of public equity must be allowed to make their own decisions. If every deal must be submitted to higher authorities for approval, many opportunities will be lost, putting state interests at a disadvantage.

Then, how should the holders of public equity be dealt with when they are allowed to make their own decisions and their decisions bring harm to state interests? These so-called "harms to state interests" refer to losing money in transactions and reducing the ratio of public equity. Regarding the first situation, it has been discussed above. There bound to be gains and losses in stock market transactions. As long as the losses are caused not by violating relevant regulations and being derelict of duty, but by inexperience or misjudgment, those who are responsible should not be punished just on the basis of one bad deal; rather they should be allowed to "learn to swim by swimming." Otherwise, no one will dare to act as the holder of state equity and trade in the stock market. As for the second situation, one should not just look at one side of the picture. On the one hand, it is true that the amount of state equity has been reduced. Yet, on the other, the shares sold have generated large quantities of funds. In the final sense, this should not be regarded as a harm to state interests. Even the individuals who buy state equity will not be able to control the enterprises, because, according to current stipulations, the names of people who hold more than 50 percent of a shareholding company's openly issued shares, as well as the top ten shareholders of the company, must be disclosed. In this situation, preventive measures can be taken beforehand. In addition, the ratio of shares to be held by single individuals in a company can be limited. Moreover, to circulate state equity in the market not only means allowing individuals to buy state equity; it also means that state-owned enterprises and the state can buy individual shares. With the three barriers, one should not worry about enterprises being controlled by individuals.

Section 2 Models of Market Circulation for Public Equity

1. The Best Model: Allowing Public Equity and Private Shares to Be Traded Freely on the Same Market.

With regard to models of market circulation for public equity, there are roughly four suggestions: One calls for free transactions of both public equity and private shares in the same market. The advantages of this model are: As corporate investors, units holding public equity can make wiser investment decisions than individual investors; this is conducive to curbing the speculative nature of the market and bringing into full play the guiding role of public equity in the secondary market. In addition, a unified market and unified prices make market management easier. The second suggestion is to separate the market for public equity and the market for private shares. This suggestion is put forth because some people worry that, due to the impact of market supply-demand relations, circulating public equity and private shares at the same market might gradually reduce the ratio of public equity. The third suggestion is to establish a "double-track and yet interlinked" stock market mechanism. It means that, in principle, transactions in public equity and in private shares are separate, but that government departments in charge can, when stock prices soar, give approval to enterprises with high public equity ratios to sell part of public equity to private shareholders, thus regulating the market. When stock prices fall sharply, government departments can allow publicly owned units to take in some private shares with their own funds. On the one hand, this practice can prevent the reduction of the ratio of public equity; on the other, it can strengthen the capacity of government departments in regulating the stock market through economic means. The fourth suggestion is to sell public equity in the form of B shares, which can be bought by overseas investors with foreign exchange.

To choose from among the four models, the key is to see which option can maintain the holding position of public equity and at the same time bring into full play the role of public equity in the stock market. At present, most experts tend to adopt the first model. But, as the question of the performance of state equity covers a wide range of topics and produces a widespread impact, it is therefore necessary to, while ensuring the optimized distribution of state-owned assets (and maintaining or increasing their value), give full consideration to the capacity of the secondary market and maintain the stability of the stock market. For instance, the state should, in line with the relative importance of each shareholding company in the national economy, decide its proprietary ratios at that company. At the same time, the method of fixing quotas on an annual basis should be adopted for public equity transactions on the stock market so as to enforce a total amount control; in line with state industrial policies and the specific conditions on the stock market, the listing of public equity should be carried out in a gradual manner and the time limit should be flexible.

Some experts point out the drawbacks of the second model: Two independent markets and two lines of prices may cause frictions in stock market performance. For instance, the Securities Exchange Quotation System is not handling equity right transactions in corporate equity, and the prices listed are much lower than those listed in the market for private shares. If an enterprise is listed both in the market for private shares and in the market for public equity, there will be two markets and two prices for the same kind of shares. This will bring many contradictions in stock market performance. For example, when an enterprise decides to expand an issue, it must have two prices. As a result, investing in the same kind of shares of the same enterprise will be different. Therefore, public equity should be circulated and it should be circulated in the same market with private shares. As for how to maintain the dominant position of public equity when it is put in market circulation, it can be dealt with in practical market performance.

After public equity is listed in the market, in order to guarantee the state's proprietary position, two solutions can be adopted. On the one hand, the state can fix an appropriate holding ratio for a given variety of enterprises, such as 25 percent, or 30 percent, or even higher. On the other, the equity can be thinly scattered. For instance, it can be stipulated that the ratio of non-public equity cannot exceed a certain percentage; this will make it possible for the state to maintain its control over enterprises. Other experts suggest setting up some holding companies to take care of state equity, to list public equity by installments and at different times so as to avoid causing shocks to the stock market.

Some experts suggest that the market circulation of public equity can be in several forms: The first is directional circulation, that is, circulation among holders of public equity. The second is circulation according to certain set ratios, that is, to lay aside a certain proportion of public equity for circulation in the market. The third is to allow the expanded part(new issues) to circulate.

2. Hainan Can Take the Lead in Establishing a Comprehensive National Stock Exchange.

The separation of public equity from private shares will lead to a lopsided development of the circulation market. Therefore, it is imperative to unite the market for public equity with the market for private shares. Experts suggest to first build a comprehensive national stock exchange in Hainan.

The exchange of private shares and public equity on two different markets at two different prices is disadvantageous to the development of the market. A stock exchange for comprehensive share transactions can be built on a trial basis in Hainan. At the exchange, both types of shares can be listed at the same prices and according to the same standards; and private and corporate equity also can be exchanged.

Hainan has the following special conditions for the experiment: (1) Hainan is a big special economic zone and enjoys more flexible policies; it has been charged with the job of experimenting in economic reform. (2) Over the past few years, the shareholding system has been smoothly introduced in Hainan. (3) Enterprises that have adopted the shareholding system are mostly newly established ones without any historical burdens. Take the few Hainan enterprises that have been listed at the Shenzhen Stock Exchange for example. All of them were established just a few years ago. They follow the shareholding system and exhibit little influence of the planned economy. (4) Hainan has an ample supply of funds, because fairly large amounts of funds — from enterprises and institutions as well as individuals throughout the country — have flowed to Hainan. (5) Hainan enjoys a better environment in terms of the market economy. For instance, limits on prices have been basically lifted and a new type of social security program has been established and put into effect. This represents a great advantage. (6) The equity structure of shareholding enterprises in Hainan is more rational and covers very wide areas. At present, of the total equity capital of all shareholding enterprises in the province, state equity constitutes only 2.7 percent. The equity capital comes from more than 20 provinces, autonomous regions and municipalities directly under the central government, as well as over ten ministries and commissions under the State Council — it has gone beyond the province to become national in significance. At the same time, In directional fund raising, both private and foreign-funded enterprises not only can be involved but also serve as the founders. (7) The Standing Committee of the Hainan Provincial People's Congress took the lead in the country to enact the *Provisions Regarding the Management of Limited-Liability Companies* in August 1992. This document has played an important role in helping the shareholding system experimentation go smoothly. (8) According to statistics available, of the total volume of transactions via the National Automated Quotation System and the Chinese People's Bank's system for transactions of corporate equity, Hainan took the largest share in listed corporate equity, accounting for 50 percent or even more of the total volume of transactions via the two systems. That is to say, corporate equity from Hainan came to the market earlier and the volume of transactions is larger than any other place. Therefore, it is comparatively easy to experiment in comprehensive share transactions in Hainan.

The circulation of corporate equity is a very important issue. It is not only the most important and immediate issue in the development of China's stock market but also the most crucial issue in determining whether China's stock market can influence and promote the country's financial system reform. It can also be said to be an issue vital to the development of China's market economy. If the problem of corporate equity circulation is not solved, the marketization of state-owned assets management cannot be solved. No fundamental change can be effected regarding the government's macroeconomic control, and thus it will lack the foundation for solving important problems in the march towards the establishment of a market economy. Therefore, we must view the issue from the angle of the overall market economy rather than just from the angle of the stock market or securities market. The solution of the problem will mean the solution of a problem that has widespread significance.

Viewing the circulation of corporate equity in the country as a whole, corporate equity circulates slowly and in small amounts. This situation calls for change. The circulation of corporate equity must be accelerated.

At the same time, further breakthroughs are needed in the stipulations of current policies regarding the circulation and equity structure of corporate equity. Hainan has made a breakthrough in the current policy concerning directional fund raising because the National People's Congress has invested Hainan with special legislative power. Other places do not have this power. These problems, if not solved, are barriers to equal competition in the market economy and are not in conformity with the principles of the market economy.

Section 3 Supporting Measures for the Circulation of Public Equity

It is by no means a simple project to bring public equity to the market. Comparatively speaking, the circulation of public equity in the market is more complicated than that of private shares, while the circulation of state equity is again more complicated than that of corporate equity. To list and circulate public equity in the market, attention must be paid to tackling the following problems:

1. The Owner of a Public Equity Property Right Must Be Clear and the Rights and Interests of Shareholders Must Be Protected.

To list and circulate public equity in the market, it is necessary to tackle first the issue of the ownership of equity rights. Without the owner, it will be impossible to exercise equity rights. It is comparatively easy to decide the owner of corporate equity; for state equity, it is rather difficult. To overcome the difficulty, it is important to distinguish the owner of state-owned assets from the owner of state equity, and distinguish the administrator of state-owned assets and the manager of state equity. Under the current conditions in China, it is rather difficult and complicated to clarify the rights of the various government departments over state-owned assets. Thus, there are certain difficulties in deciding the owner of state-owned assets.

However, this does not mean it is impossible to decide the owner of state equity. The ownership of state equity can be in two forms. One is to exercise equity right in the capacity of a administrator of state-owned assets. In this situation, the owner of state equity is actually government departments, and the determination of the ownership of state equity and of state-owned assets becomes the same thing. Hence, it is rather hard to determine the owner of state equity. Even if it is solved, it is still difficult for the owner of state equity to achieve independence and for the state equity to enter the market.

The other form is to make the owners of state equity exercise their equity right in the capacity of managers of state equity. In this situation, the owners of state equity are not government departments but institutions that manage the state-owned equity capital. In this way, it is relatively easy to tackle the problems of independence for the owner of the property right for state equity and the owner for the listing of state equity. The concrete forms of such ownership can be state-owned assets managing companies, investment companies, group companies, etc. They hold the state capital entrusted to them by government departments, enjoy the full rights of shareholders and, proceeding from self-interests, take care of the input structure and working returns of state capital in various industries and enterprises. At the same time, they form a mechanism which cuts the direct administrative links between government departments and enterprises and curbs government interference in enterprise management — a situation which has been described as "inseparation between government administration and enterprise management." It is a basic requirement for state equity to enter the market to establish state equity management organizations that differ from government departments and can independently exercise shareholders rights.

2. The Equity Right for Public Equity Must Be Scattered.

Over-concentration of equity right is a major feature regarding public equity at present. In the equity structure of all listed companies so far, the ratio held by state equity runs as high as 60-70 percent; the lowest is also over 20 percent; and the ratio held by a single legal person can be as high as 30-50 percent. Over-concentration of equity right is of course conducive to maintaining a holding position by the owner of public capital, but not conducive to the performance of the stock market and the listing of public equity in the market. One basic reason is that, if there is an over-concentrated equity right, public equity will easily manipulate the market once it comes to the market: selling in large amounts when stock prices go up to reap benefits from stock price differentials, and buying in large amounts when prices go down to incease holding rights. In this way, large amounts of private capital in the stock market will fall into the hands of state or legal persons in no time, eventually resulting in the disappearance of private shares and the end of the stock market.

The holding position of public capital and over-concentration of equity right are two different problems and they should not be treated as one and handled with simplified policies. In other words, it is necessary to guarantee the holding position of public capital but not necessary to concentrate the equity right in the hands of a few shareholders. It is entirely possible to scatter the equity right to several dozen, several hundred and even several thousand legal person shareholders (state-owned shares management organizations are also legal persons). On the one hand, the scattering of equity right of public equity will not weaken the holding position of public equity in the listed companies; rather, it will be conducive to giving public equity and private shares equal rights and interests in the enterprises. On the other hand, it is conducive to preventing public equity from manipulating the market and reaping great benefits from stock price differentials. It also helps remove the fear of private shareholders about public equity and makes public equity and private shares equal in the market.

Two measures must be adopted to effect the scattering of equity right for public equity. First, in enterprise reorganization, the state equity generated from state-owned assets must not be simply concentrated in the hands of one or a few state-owned assets management organizations; the equity right should be scattered in line with the requirements of stock market transactions. The formation of corporate equity should also be amply scattered. Second, the shares owned by company founders must subject to some time limits in being listed and traded in the stock market (for instance, it could be stipulated that shares owned by a founder are allowed to be transferred one year after the company goes into operation). After the shares are allowed to be traded, their ratio should also be limited within a specified period of time (for instance, six months after they are listed in the market).

3. Equality in the Formation Mechanism for Public Equity and Private Equity.

At present, a considerable degree of inequality exists in terms of the equity formation mechanism between state equity and corporate equity on the one hand and private shares on the other.

The equity of state equity and corporate equity among the founders' shares is mostly formed according to the net book value or the nominal value of new capital inputs, while the equity for private shares in society is mainly formed through issuance at a premium. On the one hand, this equity formation mechanism makes it possible, in the process of equity formation, for public equity to freely reap the real benefit produced by inputs made by private investors in the listed companies. On the other, it makes the trading in private shares start at high price which will not come down easily. For public equity to be listed and traded in the market, it is imperative that it should be traded at the same price as private shares of the same category. Administrative power and policy promises cannot become a pretext for government departments to reap the founding profits. Similarly, to maintain and increase the value of state-owned assets should in no way become the legal responsibility of the listed companies, because the companies should guarantee the investment interests of all shareholders rather than just satisfy the demands of certain shareholders, and, objectively speaking, the operation of any enterprise entails risk.

4. Adopting the Shareholding System by Former Enterprises, Earnestly Reappraising Their Shares and Assets, and Granting Equity Equality and Offering Same Rights for Same Category of Shares.

In current efforts to introduce the shareholding system in existing enterprises, the reappraised value of state-owned assets is often lower than their real value. In reappraising the value of the state-owned assets, the value of some factors, such as that of real estate, property rights and commercial credit, is often estimated too low, or does not count at all (the value of land, which may be located in commercially golden areas, is sometimes not calculated at all). This irregular practice naturally compels state-owned assets management departments to demand equity rights for state equity at state-set prices or cut-rate prices, resulting in the problem of ambiguous distinction between property right and ownership, and may lead to an undesireable situation whereby the various parties bid against each other to obtain the equity right. It also sows the seeds of new problems, including the problem of unequal rights for the same category of shares. Therefore, to solve the problem of state equity, it is necessary first of all to accurately appraise the value of state-owned assets and shares.

It is not only necessary to accurately appraise the value of state-owned tangible assets but also give rational value to state-owned incorporeal assets, such as patents and trademarks. Only in this way, will it be possible to ensure that the state-owned assets suffer no losses, thus ensuring the establishment of the shareholding system in the standard manner. On the basis of accurately and rationally reappraising the value of various sorts of assets, it is necessary to adopt the principle of same prices for the same category of shares regardless of the position of the would-be shareholders. No matter what a form the issue of shares adopts — at premium or at par price, the state must convert the reappraised assets into shares according to the issue prices.

5. **Establishing and Improving the Stock Market Legal System, Upholding the Principle of Being "Open, Fair and Equal" and Replacing "Administration by Man" with "Administration by Law."**

This includes disclosing all relevant stock market information, banning deals among insiders and all forms of market manipulation, preventing power deals in the stock market and promoting strict observation of the law. To this end, it is necessary to enact as soon as possible the Securities Law, Law Regarding Securities Exchange, Investment Law, Brokerage Law and other related laws. In addition, a trained contingent which strictly enforces the law must be established.

Public equity entering the market also gives rise to a series of other problems, such as problems in ideological understanding and problems regarding the functions of state equity. In terms of ideological understanding, one problem needs to be clarified: ensuring the dominant role of public ownership. First, it depends on the ratio of publicly owned capital in the total capital of the national economy; and second, it depends on the vigor of the publicly owned capital. It neither demands nor it is possible to demand that state capital always maintains a holding ratio in every enterprise. Therefore, it is impossible to directly copy the macroeconomic proportional relations to every microeconomic unit (enterprise). With regard to the functions of state equity, it has two tasks — maintaining market stability and reaping economic benefits, with the emphasis on reaping economic benefits. Therefore, state-owned shares exert regulatory and stabilizing functions in the stock market, yet the full play of these functions also depends on the functions of non-equity state capital in the securities market, such as the amount, structure and interest rates of national debts, as well as their ratio and comparative returns against shares. In short, after public equity enters the stock market, one cannot pin all hopes of market regulation and stabilization on it; rather, various monetary means should be employed to achieve this end.

Public equity entering the market is an important step for the stock market to play its role of efficiently allocating investment resources in society. Its success or failure or its pace are directly related to the change in the enterprise operational mechanism, the change of the macroeconomic regulatory mechanism, the growth of the stock market as well as the development of the national economy. Therefore, it should be promoted actively, carefully and steadily; attention should be given to synchronize it with other reform strategies.

Chapter 5
Government Roles in the Securities Market

Section 1 Functions of the Government in the Development of the Securities Market

Judging by the experience of many developing countries, the government plays an important role in both the formation and improvement of the securities market. China is a country that has an economic system characterized by a planned economy and centralized authority. To shift from a planned economy to market economy, particularly in the development and improvement of the securities market, the government's role and influence are of vital importance.

The government's duties in forming and influencing securities market are multifaceted. Apart from adopting various measures to directly promote the development of the securities market, it should also create a sound macroeconomic environment for enterprises to earn profits. A poor macroeconomic environment and the absence of sound industrial policies will not be able to produce profitable enterprises, which are indispensable to the development of the securities market.

The basic duties of the government in forming and influencing the securities market can be summarized as follows:

1. Protection of Basic Property Rights.

When people buy securities, they actually buy a kind of property right, which is something with value. The ownership over such value should be protected by property right and contract laws. Obviously, when the property rights contained in the securities are transferred, if the right is not clear or if it does not exist at all, the buyer of the securities is cheated.

2. Transparency of Trading and Other Procedures.

This is also a basic duty of the government, because it supposes that the securities market is conducive to economic development, the decisions of investors in buying or selling securities are made on their own initiative, it is then necessary to let people know which enterprises are successful and which are not. If investors' decisions are not based on sound information, these decisions are like gambling. The accuracy and transparency of information and transparency of market performance are all necessary. Only in this way, can the stock market benefit economic development, and help capital flow to successfully managed and profitable enterprises. Investors need to know who the effective and ineffective managers are. Therefore, providing correct information is an important role of the government; this is different from interference, such as when the government decides prices and gets involved in price changes. In the march towards the market economy, the government should refrain from doing such things. These decisions should be left to those who trade in the market.

3. Protecting Investors from Harms Caused by Unfair Practices by Intermediaries and Insiders, Market Manipulation and Loss of Control of Externalities; Protecting the Confidence of Securities Market Investors.

It is extremely important to protect investors from harms caused by securities market intermediaries. In the securities market, investors should be confident that the money and securities they entrust to brokers are under protection.

On the stock and securities markets, the duties of the government, in general, are to establish the market structure, rather than to be involved too deeply in market performance. The market can operate by itself, and it is the people themselves and not the government who make decisions in the market. Therefore, the government should only be involved in the establishment of structure, that is, establishing the infrastructure for exchanges in shares and other securities and setting the goals for software building. The government should seek to build a securities market that is efficient, fair and stable. Of the three, efficiency is the most important, because the government hopes to have a securities market that can contribute to economic development. To certain extent, the efficiency of the market can effectively regulate securities (through its price mechanism) and effectively raise funds. This is the key reason why the securities market is conducive to economic development.

In a country where the securities market is just starting to develop, it is hard to imagine the government not intervening in the market at all. In all developing countries, governments intervene much in the stock markets. There are good reasons for this: (1) The rules and regulations are experimental and still do not have legal force; (2) both investors and people employed in the securities business are immature; and (3) the markets have just begun to develop and many things are absent. To develop the securities market under socialism is much more complicated than to do so under capitalism. Therefore, it is unwise to discard government intervention and rely entirely on the self-regulation by market intermediaries at the very beginning. Those harmed will be the people, and possibly the state and the collectives. It might even endanger the whole system.

In an emerging securities market, intervention by the government is necessary. However, it is far more complicated in practice to determine what kind of government intervention can achieve the best results. Take the stock market in Shenzhen for example. In 1990, stock price in Shenzhen plunged into intermittent sharp rises and falls. Under this situation, the Securities Market Leading Group under the Shenzhen city government decided to adopt the rise- and fall-halt system, that is, to artificially impose daily a limit on the range of stock price rising or falling. Contrary to one's expectation, the good-intentioned measure produced the opposite result. The reason, according to the *Financial Times*, was that the decisions made by share buyers and sellers were entirely based on their stock market trend predictions. The stock investors' predictions produced a natural regulatory influence on the stock market. The artificial price-limit measures created a situation whereby investors all drew the same conclusion. When prices soared, people would draw the conclusion, because of the man-made price-limit measure, that "stock prices will certainly continue to soar." Then they competed with each other to buy shares. When prices fell, people would deduce that "stock prices will continue to fall." And then they would vie with one another to dump shares. This robotic mentality of the investors further aggravated market fluctuations. The good intention of the government did not win support of the stock investors, either. Moreover, when the falling trend in the Shenzhen stock market seemed to drag on, the rise- and fall-halt system had not only failed to check the bearish trend but became an obstacle to possible stock price reactionary rises. Finally, the Shenzhen city government, after repeated discussions, decided to gradually abolish the rise-and fall-halt system in June 1991 and replace it with an open price policy.

From the description above, it can be seen that though the government's measures to correct abnormal stock price fluctuations is well-intended, its intervention is heavy-handed. Ideally, after the shares are listed and traded in the market, the government departments in charge should devote their primary attention to ensuring fair and legitimate trading and market operations, rather than pay too much attention to price levels. In the economic sphere, artificial efforts often play a role of a double-bladed sword: while they solve some problems, they create others.

Section 2 The Government's Policy Choices in the Development of Securities Market

1. It is Necessary to Find the Right Balance Between Market Forces and Government Intervention and Make Efforts to Handle Well the Contradiction Between Government Supervision and Market Development.

Securities market is a free market institution, but what it does is often affected by the direct and indirect actions of the government. On the one hand, this has the advantage of equipping the government with tools to achieve its policy goals for the supervision and development of the securities market. On the other, it has the disadvantage that government actions can easily diminish or negate the positive contribution the securities market can make in regulating the allocation of investment resources. It is therefore especially important in the securities market to find the right balance between market forces and government intervention and to ensure that government involvement is well-targeted and efficiently executed.

Government intervention in the securities market typically takes two forms, and this can bring about conflicts in the goals pursued by the government. These two forms of intervention are supervisory and developmental. The government may supervise the market through laws and regulations, with the goal of ensuring that it operates in a fair, efficient and stable manner. At the same time, it may also implement policies designed to develop the securities market through incentives, with the goal of ensuring that capital raisers and investors have access to trading and trade-related facilities adequate for their needs.

There are conflicts between these two forms of regulation. For instance, if the government encourages an expansion in the ownership of company stock, it will contradict the goal of encouraging the accumulation of savings. Another example is the conflict between the goal of developing the market by encouraging companies to offer their securities to the public and the disincentive to go public created by the regulatory goal of fairness which requires extensive information disclosure by such companies.

These conflicts highlight the potential for securities market supervisory authorities to lose track of their mission and goals. The supervisory function requires management personnel with a strong sense of commitment, as well as specific technical skills. It may not fit well with the role of market development which requires a different corporate culture, one which emphasizes market-oriented creativity, and an open, facilitative mind.

Some countries deal with this problem by splitting the two roles between two agencies. This can lead to a lack of coordination and bureaucratic jealousies as well as increased rigidity in both agencies. Other countries combine them in one agency. This requires close attention to defining the agency's mission and goals.

Whatever administrative arrangement is adopted, government efforts to develop the securities market are by no means assured of success. There is the potential to distort or derail the securities market's course of development just as much as there is the potential to facilitate it. Success or failure depends on the type and intensity of the intervention.

Where the government has the intention of generating rapid securities market development, there is a tendency to intervene more extensively and forcefully in order to force "hothouse" growth. This intense intervention increases the likelihood of distorting the path of securities market development because it accelerates growth and change ahead of the real demands of capital raisers and investors. And apart from the question of intensity, success or failure of government intervention also depends on whether the intervention is well-targeted and whether the measures for the intervention are fully executed. Inappropriate or badly executed government intervention can impose unnecessary costs on the private sector or add a misleading factor to decision making by capital raisers and investors.

2. When a Country's Securities Market Is Absent or Small, the Government Needs to Intervene Directly in the Securities Market and Create a Sound Policy Environment to Stimulate Its Development.

Direct government intervention includes:

— Reduce capital raising costs by offering a significant tax advantage to companies which go public and list their equity securities;

— Increase the stock of tradeable securities to provide market scale by commanding that all companies with a capital value of more than US$1 million and a five-year business history must list their securities;

— Reduce transaction costs by fixing brokerage commission

fees at a low level; and

— Lower the direct cost of securities market infrastructure by financing and operating the stock exchanges directly by the government.

To directly stimulate the development of the market, it is necessary to alter policies in the following areas, which have an impact on the securities market:

— Put a cap on the amount of credit commercial banks are allowed to provide to enterprises and lower the effective interest rate on bank deposits so as to push both capital raisers and investors to the securities market;

— Stimulate liquidity in the securities market by applying a lower or zero capital gains tax to trading profits while taxing other unearned income; and

— Create a less restrictive policy environment with the intention of facilitating the growth of the securities market; maintain a sound and stable macroeconomy, keep interest rates low but positive; and gear up with foreign investment rules and procedures to facilitate portfolio investment from abroad.

It is clear that the government has a range of tools available to stimulate securities market growth. But the question is when should it use those tools and which ones. If a significant number of profitable enterprises are near the limit of their borrowing capacity and their expansion is being constrained by the high cost of capital-raising in the securities market, policies which facilitate market growth and meet the needs of the companies can be considered. But, if business profitability is too low, this kind of government intervention would be ineffective or distort investment decisions. Therefore, the best developmental option is to create a favorable investment environment for the securities market.

Let us assume for the moment that it is appropriate to consider the first option because profitable enterprises are restricted by market deficiencies from raising capital needed. Experts analyzed the choices and questions that arise in this situation.

On the supply side, there are two ways to increase the number of companies listed on the stock exchange: (1) provide a tax incentive; and (2) institute a size-related regulation. Similarly on the demand side, two options are suggested: (1) keep transaction costs low by holding down brokerage fees; and (2) subsidize the cost of market infrastructure to increase transaction efficiency.

The first suggestion on the supply side has some merits because it seeks to make it more attractive for companies to consider diversified financing but leaves the decision-making to the companies. The negatives of this suggestion are that it will mean a revenue reduction for the government and will foster an excessively tax-driven decision by companies.

The second suggestion on the supply side has little to be recommended because compulsion to list bears no relation to the needs of the companies to raise capital in the securities market. This is a policy focused on expanding the securities market rather than on allowing the securities market to expand to meet the needs of capital raisers and investors.

On the demand side, the first suggestion is not likely to be beneficial. It proposes to constrain transaction costs by holding down brockerage fees. It thereby sets the scene for costs to be shifted elsewhere by brokers — possibly to increase insurance fees which will raise the cost of listing companies; or for the proliferation of under-funded and consequently inefficient brokerage operations.

The second demand-side suggestion is more positive because it facilitates but does not force market development. It focuses on the provision of infrastructure, which is an appropriate role for the government when such costs are high. But, it could be an expensive undertaking initially and quite a drain on government revenue. This strategy also requires government personnel with a high degree of technical sophistication and institution-building know-how; at present, people with this kind of background are in short supply.

So, when the government adopts policies to intervene in the development of the securities market, it should give careful consideration to the possible outcomes, intended or unintended.

Section 3 The Government's Policy Options for Securities Market Supervision

There are four basic forms of securities market regulatory activity — prudential, protective, organizational and structural.

1. Prudential Controls

Prudential controls establish capital adequacy requirements for intermediaries and a system for monitoring and enforcing them. They impose direct capital costs justified on the basis of the need to overcome market externalities, such as possible systemic contagion from the financial failure of an intermediary.

2. Protective Controls

Protective controls establish a framework for relations between intermediaries and their clients and between small and large investors. They emphasize information disclosure, clarity of contractual relationship and strict fiduciary responsibility. Protective controls seek to protect the smallest and/or least sophisticated investors.

3. Organizational Controls

Organizational controls provide for the establishment and operation of such organizations as stock exchanges, clearing houses and market information systems. The aim is to allow for competition in the market for providing these services but they do impose entry criteria, such as financial soundness and technical competence of the service provider, so that the stability of the system as a whole may be protected.

4. Structural Controls

Structural controls allow the government to manage the overall balance and shape of the securities market through such mechanisms as restrictions on foreign ownership of intermediaries, on the type of activity an intermediary may engage in, and on the specifications of the instruments which may be traded.

These four forms of regulatory activity translate in practice to the performance of a diverse range of functions: rule making; market monitoring and investigation; prosecution of breaches of the law; examination and approval of prospectuses and other corporate documents; auditing of financial statements and other documents of intermediaries; and supervision of the operational and financial stability of stock exchanges, clearing houses and other types of market service providers.

The practical implementation of these laws and general policies through the performance of these functions is likely to produce a great impact on the efficiency, fairness and stability of the market because a great deal of discretionary power is often involved. These functions must be carried out in situations of policy conflict and fluidity.

Securities market supervision is labor intensive and its success relies on the commitment, judgement and skill of the personnel involved. Extensive training and re-training are required to achieve the necessary level of professionalism. Also essential is an organizational structure and corporate culture which ensures high ethical and technical standards. This is clearly a long-term task for many developing countries.

Section 4　Standardization and Legislation of Securities Market

1. The Degree of Management Standardization in the Securities Market Indicates Its Developmental Level.

The degree of standardization of a securities market's performance and management serves as a major indicator showing its level of maturity. It is also an important condition for conducting macroeconomic regulation, raising market efficiency and winning the public confidence. At present, the level of standardization of China's securities market is generally very low. Moreover, there are large gaps between different places. Market performance lacks comprehensive legal guarantees because market rules and regulations are not complete and unified. As a result, some unhealthy phenomena have surfaced in the issuance and trading of securities. Many systems and measures are not in accord with international conventions, producing an unfavorable impact on China's efforts in securities issuing overseas and its movement towards internationalization.

China's pattern of issuing securities needs to be improved. Issuing by lottery and queuing up for purchases not only pushes up the cost of issuing but tends to harm the principle of being open, fair and equal. Securities dealing organizations have failed to play the roles of guiding investment behavior of the public as well as shaping and fostering the market. The self-regulation mechanism of the securities market still lacks a set of well-knit systems.

2. Incomplete Laws and Regulations — an Outstanding Problem for the Securities Market.

Without proper laws, confusion and chaos can easily occur in the securities market. Although the state has enacted a number of legal documents for the securities market, such as *Circular on Strengthening Management of Share Certificates and Bonds* by the State Council, *Provisions of Shanghai Municipality on Management of Securities* by the Shanghai Municipal Government, *Provisional Regulations of Shenzhen City on Management of the Issuing and Trading of Securities* by the Shenzhen City Government, etc., much still needs to be done.

To help China's securities market embark on the road of sound development, it is imperative to standardize all actions in the issuing and trading of securities. In other words, there must be laws for people to follow, the enforcement of the laws must be strict and those who violate the laws must be dealt with. In terms of the country as a whole, the Securities Law, the Accounting System of Joint-Stock Enterprises and some other supporting cardinal laws have not yet been enacted. Without strict securities market legislation, it will be hard to exercise effective supervision over black market activities, cheating, price manipulation and profiteering by securities management personnel, employees in the securities business as well as Party and government functionaries. To protect the interests of investors and promote the sound development of the securities market, the behaviors of market actors must be codified in law.

Some experts hold it is necessary to unify the rules of listing securities, rules of competition and rules of securities management that exist im different places. It is necessary to draw a strict demarcation between bonds and share certificates and protect the development of the stock market. It is necessary to ensure competition on an equal footing among capital raisers, among investors and between capital raisers and investors. This will help make the competition mechanism play the roles of balancing fund supply and demand, regulating the investment choices of the general public, adjusting the securities structure and reducing the phenomena of blind competition and segmented competition. It is necessary to remove business performance barriers and make business activities standard. At the same time, it is necessary to improve self-regulation of and social supervision over the securities trade by strengthening the organizational establishment of self-regulatory institutions and legislative work, clarifying the functions and responsibilities of these organizations, as well as concrete requirements for them. It is necessary to organically combine macroeconomic control by the government and self-regulation of the securities trade by bringing into active play social supervision by securities administrative departments, accounting firms, auditing offices and the general public. In addition, it is necessary to strengthen the training of securities trade personnel, improve communication facilities and operational means, and publicize information about securities so as to enhance knowledge about financial investment (and its inherent risks) in the business community and the general public. In general, efforts must be made to strengthen legislative work, maintain orderly performance of the securities market and accelerate the pace of internationalization of the market.

3. Legislation Is Necessary to Standardize Joint-Stock System and the Performance of the Securities Market.

In legislative work, it is necessary to solve the following three problems: (1) How to maintain the predominant role of public ownership in shareholding enterprises; (2) how to introduce standardization to the shareholding system and securities issuing and trading; and (3) how to prevent some people from using the shareholding system experiment process to seek personal gains. To this end, enacted laws should include clear stipulations regarding the reappraisal of the value of state-owned assets as well as the issuance of new shares, so as to ensure the principles of being open, fair and equal and the active and steady expansion of the shareholding system experiment. At the same time, it is necessary to stipulate in law that the state should maintain a predominant position in key enterprises and monopolized industries which are directly related to the national economy and people's livelihood.

It is necessary to use legislation to prevent serious disparities in distribution. At present, China should enact laws to encourage securities investors' enthusiasm and, at the same time, restrict excessive speculation on the part of investors who live on capital incomes. Levying transaction tax or stamp duties is one way to deal with this situation. Taxation policies are an extremely important means to regulate the securities market.

It is necessary to establish clear qualifications for securities investors and set legal restrictions on the amount of securities to be held by single shareholders. In line with international conventions, China should stipulate in law that people employed in the securities industry and workers in related departments must not buy and sell shares. The law should also include restrictive stipulations on the amount of shares held by single shareholders as well as stipulations regarding the qualifications for investors in securities, so as to effectively prevent deals by insiders and monopolies in securities transactions.

It is necessary to establish a national unified securities market through the enactment of laws. The segmentation of the securities market causes wanton black market activities and stimulates profit-seeking speculative activities. It also makes it difficult for the securities market to accurately reflect the relation between supply and demand and the rational flow of funds. At present, China's securities market is still in its initial stage: it is quite scattered and lacks mutual connection. To improve its condition, it is necessary to reform the current securities market regulatory system as well as its operational pattern. This will gradually establish a complete series of unified market regulatory rules and a supporting legal system as well as an effective macro-balance system. Of course, the formation of a unified national securities market also depends on state policies, the development of the shareholding economy as well as its improved position in the national economy as a whole.

It is necessary to enact laws governing the establishment of a securities investment taxation system. To mitigate the phenomenon of polarization caused by securities investment, China should accelerate its pace of legislative work and make clear stipulations concerning taxing income from interests, dividends and capital gains. The tax rates should be appropriate, not only based on conditions in China but also taking into consideration tax rates in both developed and developing countries.

4. It is Necessary to Boldly Learn from Other Countries' Experience in Securities Legislative Work and Strictly Enforce Laws.

The legal framework for the securities market covers the organization and control over limited-liability companies. It includes these facets: control over the issuance of shares (including underwriting forms as well as the examination and approval of issues); control over securities dealers (including qualifications and codes of conduct); the administration of the securities exchange market (including the organization and performance of the market, supervision over stock exchanges, transactions in securities, standards for listing and transaction restrictions); legal liabilities (including civil and criminal responsibilities, particularly those connected with open notices for bidding with incomplete information about the buying and selling of securities, market manipulation and deals by insiders). Therefore, it is not every place that can establish a securities market, not any enterprise that can issue securities or list their securities once issued, and not everybody that can deal in securities. The absence of rules and law will inevitably result in confusion and undermine the normal economic order, thus hindering the goal of changing the country's enterprise management mechanism and promoting the development of the national economy through the establishment of the shareholding system. In the United States, the *Securi-*

ties Act and the *Securities Exchange Act* were enacted in 1933 and 1934 respectively. The background is the unprecedented great recession of the stock market in 1929, when large numbers of banks and securities companies went bankrupt and countless investors suffered great losses. To prevent the situation occurring again, authorities in charge enacted the laws to control the securities issue and circulation markets. Since then, the banking business has been separated from the securities business, with the aim of preventing investment in securities by abusing other people's deposits.

It is better to have laws than not have. When laws are there, it is necessary to strictly enforce them. If laws are replaced by power or corrupted by money, or if they are not strictly enforced, people would not have any confidence in laws promulgated and the dignity of the laws would be swept into the dust. In this case, having laws is not necessarily better than not having laws. If the country wishes to achieve economic development, it is imperative to standardize and institutionalize its economic management and economic operation.

Regarding the issue and exchange of share certificates for example, it does not do to only have the principle of being open, fair and equal. Efforts must also be made to fight against cheating, manipulation and insider trading. Now, China is making active efforts to establish securities market legislation. In this respect, it should boldly learn from and assimilate the experience of other countries, particularly those countries and regions where securities market laws are well developed. It makes no difference though the nature of ownership in these countries may be different than in China; the operation of the market economy and securities exchanges have common ground whether the ownership is public or private. Securities markets everywhere must have common attributes, and therefore there must be similarities in legal stipulations. China can and should learn from the experience and lessons of other countries in legislative work concerning securities, and does not have to traverse again the tortuous course others have traversed, so as to avoid unnecessary costs. Of course, while learning from other countries' experience, it is necessary for

China to enact laws that reflect its unique conditions. These laws thus enacted must both be in harmony with international conventions and have unique Chinese characteristics; also they must both maintain the dominant position of public shares and enable the shares to be exchanged on an equal and free basis. In the transactions of shares, speculation is unavoidable; but it is necessary to curb excessive speculation. For law offences in the issue and exchange of securities, it is necessary not only to investigate and affix civil responsibilities but also criminal responsibilities. If law-breaking activities, such as profiteering, are not stopped, China's securities market will not be able to embark on a course of healthy development. The confusion caused by rush purchases of share subscription certificates that occurred in August 1992 in Shenzhen is a typical example. The securities market is like a sharp sword that cuts both ways. If well operated, it will greatly promotes China's economic development; if not, it will cause economic chaos, resulting in a uncontrollable situation. Therefore, it is imperative to enact laws that include stipulations which clearly state what can and cannot be done, and also clarify the legal responsibilities.

Section 5　Bringing into Full Play the Role of the Government and Improving China's Securities Administrative System

1. Learning from Lessons Caused by Poor Government Administration.

It is impossible for the growth of the securities market to be all smooth sailing. The 1992 Chinese securities market illustrates the chaos of a young securities market: Throughout the country enterprises rushed head over heels to issue share certificates; market management was divided between many different departments, causing great confusion and arousing much worry among both Chinese and foreign experts. Experts could not understand how share certificates could be issued and listed when the laws and regulations regarding the issue and trading of share certificates were not yet enacted. Perhaps, viewed from the broad angle of reform, we have no reason whatsoever to complain after the fact about the pace of reform in China. Reform is slowly happening as the external conditions become ready. And the maturation of these conditions happens as China sails the seas of economic reform and gains experience.

Like Chinese reform in other areas, "exploring the way while forging ahead" is also the necessary model for securities market development. There is bound to be both joys and sorrows. Just when people were still euphoric over the "bullish" trend following Deng Xiaoping's speeches on a southern China inspection tour, a disastrous event occurred in the Shenzhen stock market: 1.2 million people queued, rushing to purchase a limited number of share subscription certificates. As it turned out only 10 percent of those eager buyers were able to make purchases of shares. What was even harder to understand is that this mass of contenders vied with one another to buy shares of companies they had little or no financial knowledge about. It is no wonder that some overseas experts referred to it as a "sheer gambling." As a result of this event, various bonds that were once highly rated were cold-shouldered. In order to raise the necessary funds, some enterprises competed with one another to raise the interests rates of the bonds they issued. The excessively large amount of bonds issued made the state treasury bonds — once considered "gold-rimmed bonds" — to lose their appeal.

2. Establishment of the Securities Committee and the Securities Regulatory Committee — the Securities Market Moves from Disorderliness to Orderliness.

China's economic construction experience over the past decade demonstrates that a market economy is essential to building a strong and prosperous nation and securing a high place in the ranks of the world's countries. When the flawed view that the market economy is unique to capitalism was finally discarded, a door of opportunity was opened for China's securities industry.

China must have a market economy and the securities market must develop. These call for macroeconomic control from the government so as to confine the actions of the market participants and to effectively prevent unfair practices such as monopolies, fraud, collaboration by insiders and willfully bidding up prices. This will ensure the normal operation and development of the securities market.

In order to strengthen macroeconomic control over the securities market, unify relevant policies, establish and improve the securities regulatory work system and protect the interests of all investors, the State Council established the State Council Securities Committee and the China Securities Regulatory Committee. This development indicates that China's securities market has evolved from a stage of disorderliness to a stage of orderliness. This is a goal that was accomplished in Western countries only after more than a hundred years of hardships. That it was accomplished in China in a mere few years cannot but be considered a great accomplishment.

3. Purpose of Establishing the Securities Committee and the Securities Regulatory Committee: To Bring into Full Play the Regulatory Roles of the Government over the Securities Market.

As a part of China's market economy, the securities market will play a significant role in China's future economic growth. But, it is necessary to notice at the same time that China's planned economy, formed over a long period, has not been completely transformed. With regard to the question of the securities market, which is bound to produce an impact on the overall situation, it is hard for China to establish overnight a securities administrative department independent of all other government departments.

The State Council Securities Committee, which was established at the end of 1992, is formed by leading members from 14 departments under the State Council, including the State Commission for Restructuring the Economy, the People's Bank of China, the State Planning Commission and the Ministry of Finance. Their basic duties are: Doing organizational work for drafting laws and regulations related to the securities market, studying and enacting principles, policies and rules related to the securities market; proposing and working out programs for the development of the securities market; giving guidance to, coordinating, supervising and checking the work of various localities and departments related to the securities market; and taking responsibility in the administration of the Securities Regulatory Committee.

The newly established regulatory system lays great stress on the national unity of the securities market. The regulatory responsibilities and power of local governments are strictly confined. In terms of the issuing and listing of securities, local governments can only exercise their power within the quotas for them set by the state; their power to approve enterprises for experiment in shareholding system is also strictly limited.

With regard to the experiment in the shareholding system, local enterprises are given approval by departments empowered by the governments at the provincial level or the governments of cities which draw up their own plans for economic and social development in collaboration with the departments in charge of the enterprises; enterprises controlled by the central government will be approved by the State Commission for Restructuring the Economy and the departments in charge.

At present, the Securities Committee is busy in organizing the drafting of securities laws and regulations. China is limited in financial resources and wants to prevent the exorbitant issuance of securities from harming the balance of credit funds: towards this end, the Securities Committee and the State Planning Commission have worked out a national plan for the scale of securities issuance. In addition, plans have been sketched out to involve domestic enterprises in overseas stock markets. Also, continuing the expansion of the scope of experiment on the issuance of renminbi special shares has become a great concern of securities regulatory departments. Finally, for a period to come, the Securities Committee will be faced with another task: While working to regulate the issuance of securities, active efforts will be made to experiment in issuing new varieties of securities, including investment securities, convertible securities and trust beneficiary securities, to enrich and invigorate the securities market.

Before the Securities Law, Securities Exchange Law and Law Regarding Protection of Investment in Securities are enacted, the State Council Securities Committee will work out some provisional statutes; this can both play a legally binding role in regulating the activities on the securities market and provide the National People's Congress with practical experience for finally enacting the legislations.

Compared with other ministries and commissions of the government, the China Securities Regulatory Committee is clearly different in organizational setup. It is mainly funded by the administrative charges collected from the stock exchanges, listed companies and securities dealing organizations. Nevertheless, it is the working body of the Securities Committee and shoulders all the supervisory and regulatory tasks for China's securities market.

The issue market opens one more fund-raising and investment channel, and it is the basis of the securities market. When an entity issues bonds or share certificates, it must disclose to the public its financial condition and developmental prospects with well-prepared documents and complete necessary procedures for approval. The process must be open, fair and equal. For example, regarding the issuance of share certificates when any enterprise that has been approved to issue and list shares, it must first undergo asset evaluation and financial checks by an assets-rating organization and an accounting firm approved by the Securities Regulatory Committee. The committee will examine the candidate's related reports and subscription-bidding document. Credential affirmation of securities companies and other securities dealing organizations is also a major content of the committee's regulatory capacity over the securities market. According to the *Written Instruction Regarding the Responsibilities of the China Securities Regulatory Committee* by the State Council Securities Committee in 1993, the Securities Regulatory Committee should work in collaboration with related departments in charge to check on and give approval to law and accounting firms involved in the securities business and issue licenses for operation; it should also stipulate the formulae and contents of professional reports they prepare for securities issue and trading units as well as for securities market supervisors.

Well-established and effective securities dealing organizations will not only be dealing securities for companies. Since it takes a long time for companies to prepare to turn into a shareholding company, they can also assist and give guidance to the companies regarding upgrading their finance, accounting and management procedures to reach the standards required for openly issuing and listing shares. This is not only conducive for gaining approval for listing as soon as possible, but will also favorably influence securities market growth as a whole.

The Circular on Further Strengthening Macroeconomic Control over Securities issued by the State Council points out that companies can apply for listing their shares on the stock exchanges only after their credentials have been approved by the Securities Regulatory Committee; and that, to implement the principle of being open, fair and equal in the issuance, it is necessary to publicly distribute sufficient copies of application forms for securities subscription and have the lots drawn under the supervision of public notary offices, or adopt other internationally accepted methods, so as to avoid turning the subscription certificates themselves into negotiable securities.

It is the Securities Regulatory Committee's most arduous task to supervise over and regulate the activities of the securities dealing organizations, securities clearing houses, transaction registration organizations, mutual fund management organizations and securities business employees; and to work out with departments concerned the credential requirements and code of conduct for securities business employees and see to it that they are observed. Now, with the aid of modern technology, the committee has established a monitoring system over the trading activities in the country's securities market. If a type of securities has been dull for some time and suddenly turns hot, the committee has the right to ask for an explanation. If the explanation is reasonable, such as it is caused by improved credit or returns, the matter will be closed. If it is caused by market manipulation or no obvious explanation can be provided, the committee will send people to investigate the party concerned. According to the finding of the investigation, necessary steps will be taken. In other words, through exercising its functions, the Securities Regulatory Committee hopes to help all people who are involved in securities trading understand what is and is not allowed.

When problems occurred in the securities market in the past, administrative measures were often adopted. The administrative measures which were hurriedly adopted usually attended to one thing while losing sight of others. With the establishment and gradual improvement of the new securities administrative system, when illegal speculation occurs the Securities Regulatory Committee will conduct an investigation and recommend punishment, or empower another organization to do so. Leaders of the Securities Committee and the Securities Regulatory Committee emphasized that companies that engage in unlawful speculation and people who seriously disrupt the normal order of the securities market shall be severely punished according to law.

However, experts of the Securities Regulatory Committee also clearly stated that, in enforcing supervision and control over the securities market, it is necessary to pay close attention to distinguish unlawful and lawful speculation. The former refers to when people or companies make use of their privileges and engage in insider trading or market manipulation. Such activities are not allowed in any country or stock exchange. The latter refers to when people or companies have different expectations of market returns, and buy or sell securities to earn profits. Such speculative activities are indispensable to the securities market; without them, there would be no securities market, and to ban them is tantamount to banning the securities market.

Although speculation in the latter category is rational in some sense, it must be appropriate and not excessive. Speculation to an appropriate degree is necessary for the survival of the securities market, while excessive speculation will cause great price fluctuations which will in turn scare away investors (partic-

ularly investors who pay primary attention to long-term interests). Therefore, the government must have a powerful securities supervisory and regulatory department which will lose no
time to adopt economic, legal or even administrative means to
avoid excessive speculation. In order to make timely reports to
the State Council Securities Committee on major problems crop-
ping up in the performance of the securities market and put forth
suggestions for their solution, related departments under the
Securities Regulatory Committee should carefully study the
changing trends in China's securities market and, together with
the statistics department, collect and analyze key statistics on
securities and issue them to securities business circles and the
general public.

4. Strengthening Market Self-Regulation in China's Securi-
ties Administrative System.

Of the many forms of securities administration popular in
the world nowadays, many countries and regions embrace market
self-regulation.

As securities market administrative departments, neither the
Securities Committee nor the Securities Regulatory Committee
can engage in actual securities issuing and trading themselves. As
the administrative department cannot directly take part in trading activities, its administration of the market is bound to have
some loopholes. This drawback can only be remedied by the
market self-regulation. Of course, such self-regulation by the
market does not mean the supervision and guidance by the
government can be dispensed with.

Usually, self-regulation of the securities market can accomplished in two forms.

First, it relies on the stock exchanges to control floor transactions. The stock exchanges are managed by adopting the membership system, which requires that all companies or individuals
obtain approval beforehand and become members of the stock
exchange; that all the members must observe the trading rules
and turn corresponding amounts of mortgage money; that all
members must provide the stock exchanges with their securities

business reports and statistics in line with the pre-set contents and intervals; and that the stock exchanges manage the members' stock-trading accounts.

Apart from the floor transactions discussed in the previous paragraph, there are also over-the-counter transactions. Self-regulation of over-the-counter transactions is shouldered by the securities exchange associations and other professional organizations. The China Securities Business Association founded in September 1991 is a national self-regulatory organization in the securities business, which was approved by the People's Bank of China and registered with the Ministry of Civil Affairs, and whose credentials were then affirmed by the Securities Regulatory Committee. Its major duties are to work out self-regulatory rules for the securities dealers, strengthen professional management and coordinate the relations between the members. Here, it is somewhat similar to the securities dealers' associations in other countries which, on the one hand, supervise and manage over-the-counter securities transactions, ensure that the parties concerned abide by state laws and regulations as well as the securities business codes of conduct, and see to it that over-the-counter transactions are fair and standard. And on the other hand, it serves as a bridge linking the securities administrative department of the Chinese government and the securities issuers, investors and traders.

Chapter 6
Internationalization of Securities Markets

Section 1 The Opening of Developing Countries' Securities Markets to the Outside World

1. Encourage Overseas Securities Investment and Let Securities Investors Enjoy the Same Treatment as Direct Investors.

The internationalization of securities markets in developing countries should be encouraged. Overseas securities investors should enjoy the same treatment as the direct investors. This is because: (1) Overseas securities have the potential to create an inflow of substantial amounts of stock capital. Even if a small portion of the total amount of investments by international corporate investors enters emerging markets, it is likely to constitute the bulk of the total capital in the emerging markets. (2) Overseas securities investments will stimulate the development of the domestic capital market. At the stage when the emerging markets are growing and draw in investments, they are usually in small sizes. However, foreign securities investments can agitate the development of the emerging securities markets through their increased demands of the securities. (3) More often than not, overseas securities investors are not interested in controlling the management of a company or taking a holding position. On the contrary, they prefer to use their money to buy more than one kind securities and expect satisfactory returns from their investments. For share certificates issued by any corporation, they limit their purchases to 5 percent. The purpose of overseas securities investors is, without exception, to reap the maximum returns at the minimum risk, rather than to control the corporation they invest in.

The internationalization of the emerging securities markets has the following four advantages: (1) It boosts the economic strength of the domestic stock market; (2) overseas securities investments help maintain economic growth, yet don't influence the control over the economy; (3) the direct participation of overseas investors, investment banks and brokerage companies can spur the domestic stock market to quickly improve its efficiency, accumulate experience and mature rapidly; (4) some companies in developing countries can first issue debt bonds, then convert them into exchangeable securities and finally turn them into listed share certificates. In this way, they have the chance to get involved in the international market. The funds thus pooled will be in amounts impossible to raise by relying solely on domestic sources, and the cost will be very low. With regard to the securities market in China, every effort should be made to organically coordinate the institutions, laws and regulations, finance as well as the infrastructure of the securities market, so as to keep abreast with the rapid development of other emerging markets, which are China's rivals for attracting foreign investments in the international market.

So far, more then 30 funds directed at China have been established in Hong Kong. They are aimed at investing in Chinese enterprises. The funds were first founded in Hong Kong, which then sought investment advisors on China's mainland. The absorption of foreign funds can take both the form of issuing B shares and letting Chinese enterprises list their shares directly at foreign stock exchanges. Chinese companies can also take over foreign companies or invest in them.

Some experts hold that it is highly necessary to develop China's own securities companies. It is only when a country's own securities companies have developed considerably that foreign securities companies can be let in a country or the country's own securities companies can be allowed to go abroad to set up branch companies and learn from other countries' experience. The inflow and outflow of foreign investment from the domestic securities market may produce some impact on the market prices, but this is nothing to be afraid of. Now, there is still a "China craze," as many foreign investors crave to enter China. China should take the opportunity and adopt an active attitude towards this, taking concrete, steady steps.

2. There Must Be an Upper Limit for the Ratio of Shares Held by Foreign Investors in Shareholding Enterprises.

Some developing countries welcome the coming of foreign investment on the one hand, while, on the other, set certain restrictions for its inflow, which are mainly reflected in imposing upper limits for the ratio of shares held by foreign investors in the shareholding enterprises. For instance, Malaysia stipulates that foreign investment must not exceed 30 percent of the stock of a company. Moreover, it rules that approval must be obtained from the Foreign Investment Commission when a certain foreign beneficiary has acquired 15 percent of the voting right or when all foreign beneficiaries have acquired 30 percent of the voting right of a company, or when the stock owned by foreign investors has exceeded US$5 million in value. But, if all the products of an enterprise are to be exported, the foreign investors can own 100 percent of its capital. The government of the Republic of Korea rules that foreign investors can own 15 percent of the real capital pooled by a company through issuing convertible bonds, while the maximum ratio to be held by a single foreign investor is 3 percent. Thailand stipulates that the stock controlled by foreigners in Thai companies can be as high as 49 percent. Indonesian legislation rules that foreign investors are allowed to buy as much as 49 percent of the openly listed shares of all companies. But, publicly controlled companies usually only list part of their shares, and consequently the actual ratio of securities to be acquired by foreign investors is in fact lower than the 49 percent ratio allowed by law.

So far, China has not imposed an upper limit for the ratio of stock to be held by foreign investors in shareholding companies. Nevertheless, when enterprises make efforts to absorb foreign investment, they often want to let the share of foreign investment reach 25 percent, because enterprises that operate with 25 percent foreign investment may enjoy preferential policies reserved for

Sino-foreign joint ventures. As more and more enterprises shift to the shareholding system and list their shares at the stock market, particularly when the enterprises in some important industries are listed, whether it is necessary to set an upper limit for the ratio of stock to be held by foreign investors in the enterprises is a question that calls for study.

Shanghai and Shenzhen on China's mainland also intended to let in corporate investors first via their B share issues, but the result was not as planned: both corporate and individual investors have entered the market. In Shenzhen, the individual investors outnumber corporate investors.

The opening of the securities market to the outside world also gives rise to another problem, that is, how to balance the relation between letting domestic enterprises list their shares in foreign stock markets and attracting foreign investors to invest in domestic stock markets. Some people stand for taking the development of the domestic B shares-market as the key. They feel that it is here that efficiently-managed enterprises should list their shares. They think this can achieve the dual purpose of absorbing foreign investments and promoting the development of the domestic stock market. Others hold a different view, however. They think it is necessary to select well-managed enterprises to list their shares in Hong Kong and New York, because it can not only set up a new channel for opening the country to the outside world and importing foreign funds, but also temper these enterprises in the competition of the international market. It calls for further study as to which strategy to pursue.

3. Securities Market Internationalization — the Principal Tendency in China's Securities Business Development.

The internationalization of the securities market is the fundamental pattern in China's securities business development. It requires that the country's basic market rules comply with international conventions; this enables the domestic market, through the market intermediaries, to absorb the flow of funds from the international capital market to develop the country's economy and enhance the prestige of the domestic securities business. Since

1992, China has promulgated in a succession a series of legal documents, including *Opinions Concerning the Standardization of Companies Limited by Shares* and *Opinions Concerning the Standardization of Limited-Liability Companies.* In December 1993, it promulgated *Corporation Law.* These, coupled with the rules and regulations regarding bonds and shares enacted previously (as well as the continuous amendments to these rules and regulations) have no doubt provided the groundwork necessary for China's securities business to standardize and ready itself for engaging in the international marketplace.

In the 1980s, the pattern of international capital flow in China shifted from mainly relying on raising funds through borrowing money to mainly relying on raising funds by issuing stocks. In the first stage of China's reform and opening to the outside world, the country absorbed foreign funds by mainly relying on direct investments by foreign investors and commercial loans. With the development of the securities market, particularly the emergence of the stock exchanges, and to satisfy foreign investors' demand to invest in Chinese enterprises via buying shares, absorbing foreign investment through issuing shares was put on the agenda. Generally speaking, making direct investment and buying shares can both attain the goal of investing in China and sharing in the economic growth. The results are basically the same. But, for foreign investors, buying shares is a more flexible investment method; they can better choose the direction of their investment through buying and selling shares, thus reaping greater returns. It is thus a new and more flexible channel for raising funds. Therefore, in 1991 China began issuing B shares which were directed at people abroad. It marked the first step China took to raise capital with stock rights and open the securities market to the outside world. It was basically a success.

Since 1992, China has studied the question of whether or not to allow Chinese enterprises to be directly listed in overseas stock markets. The advantages of this are: It is conducive to enhancing the international prestige of Chinese enterprises and instigating them to gear towards the international market; and through it China can learn from the experience about managing securities business overseas. Having negotiated and reached an agreement with the Hong Kong Associated Stock Exchange and the Securities Supervisory Commission, several Chinese enterprises have issued and listed H shares on the Hong Kong Associated Stock Exchange. Some Chinese enterprises have also listed in the United States. All these moves have opened up new channels in utilizing foreign funds. Nevertheless, it still calls for further studies about how large a scale should be in absorbing foreign investment through issuing shares, what the major form or forms should be, and how supervision of overseas-listed Chinese enterprises should be enforced.

By allowing foreign investors to invest in renminbi special B shares and allowing some domestic enterprises to list their shares in Hong Kong and foreign countries, it indicates that China's securities market has made an important step forward in opening to the outside world. But, many foreign investors wish to get further involved in China's securities market and some domestic enterprises wish to get involved in international securities markets. In the long run, there is the problem of how to dovetail China's securities market with the international securities market. Therefore, it is necessary to draw up a long-term plan for the further opening of China's securities market to the outside world. It is particularly so now when the management of China's securities market involves many government departments and local governments; better coordination is needed.

4. Further Internationalization of the Chinese Securities Market Calls for Marked Improvement in Currency Convertibility.

The internationalization of securities includes both the listing of Chinese companies in other countries and the further opening of China's securities market to the outside world. Thanks to the issuing and listing of B shares, a new situation has been created. At the same time, however, there are still many drawbacks in the issuance of B shares, causing problems in practical operations and policies. The further internationalization of the securities market calls for still greater progress in improving the convertibility of China's currency. One opinion stresses the importance of having the proper conditions for the convertibility of currency, such as greater export capacity and plentiful foreign exchange reserves.

Part of the above argument does not tally with international experience. Take Poland for example: A few years ago when it decided to carry out the policy of currency convertibility, it was deeply in debt, with external debts running as high as several dozen billion US dollars; moreover, it had just begun to shift to the market economy, its export capacity was very weak and it faced soaring inflation. The government of Poland adopted currency convertibility and appropriate macroeconomic policies as a means of curbing inflation, and gave a firm promise to support its currency, the zloty. Although the government did not actually have sufficient foreign exchange reserves to support its policy of currency convertibility, people had confidence that the zloty would be exchangeable for the US dollar at the set exchange rate. This confidence prevented large numbers of citizens and enterprises from rushing to change their zloty into hard currencies. So, there are different views regarding the necessary conditions for currency convertibility.

Some international organizations and experts hold that in China the conditions are now in place to speed up the pace of introducing convertibility to its currency. Yet, currency convertibility must be combined with reforms in trade and depends on overall economic stability. The convertibility of currency can start with ordinary items and then gradually be extended to capital items. In general, speeding up the course of currency convertibility is extremely important to promoting the internationalization of the securities market.

Section 2 The Impact of Foreign Securities Investment and Internationalization of Emerging Securities Markets

1. Marked Development of Emerging Securities Markets Between 1982 and 1992.

According to an investigation in 32 developing countries and regions conducted by the Capital Market Department of the International Financial Company under the World Bank in 1982, the total amount of market funds was US$66 billion, and the number of registered companies was 7,350. Malaysia occupied the first place in market funds, with US$14 billion; Brazil, second, had US$10.2 billion. Next came Taiwan and the Republic of Korea, with US$5.1 billion and US$4.4 billion respectively. That year stock transactions in these 32 countries and regions reached US$ 21 billion.

By the end of 1992, great changes had taken place. Although the world experienced two stock market crashes (one in 1987 and the other in 1990), the total capital which flowed into the emerging securities markets (taken as a whole group) ran as high as US$ 750 billion, representing a 13-fold increase. In 1982, it was estimated that the total stock capital in emerging markets accounted for 3 percent of the world's total. It doubled in 1992, reaching 7 percent. The stock exchanges in Mexico and the Republic of Korea rose to the 12th and 14th places, ranking ahead of Spain, Sweden and some other economically developed countries. The number of their listed companies also more than doubled, reaching 12,500. In 1982, the listed companies in Mexico and the Republic of Korea accounted for only 26 percent of the world's total. At present, they account for 40 percent of the some 30,000 listed companies around the world.

2. The Future for Emerging Markets.

Regarding trends for future development in emerging securities markets, some experts hold that important changes have taken place and, moreover, these changes will result in a revolution in emerging markets in the 1990s.

First, investment in securities by individuals will rapidly expand the scope of many securities markets and increase the capital flow. This phenomenon will become the core of the emerging securities markets.

Second, more and more companies will step out of the bounds of their traditional and family-like operations and to come to the domestic securities markets to raise capital. When markets are opened to international competition, companies will be forced to invest in new facilities both at home and around the world, seek export channels and conduct merges and takeovers. In the securities exchange list, the result will possibly not be manifested as dramatic rises or falls. Yet, the range of growth will indeed extend to the emerging markets.

Third, the enthusiasm to improve the environment for foreign investment will be sustained throughout the 1990s. For instance, Brazil, Pakistan, Indonesia and the Philippines have declared they have made important alterations of their related policies.

Fourth, in order to seek new stock capital sources, more and more companies of the developing countries will directly issue shares to investors in the developed countries.

Fifth, the emerging markets will rapidly mature. Many of the markets are taking pains in enacting effective rules and regulations, and establish better information systems, more advanced trading systems as well as more concentrated clearing and settlement procedures.

Just as on securities markets elsewhere, there are bound to be rises and falls on the emerging markets. Sometimes, the rises and falls will be dramatic. In the long-term point of view, however, the emerging markets can generate real benefits for the domestic economy and the foreign investors. Recently, many emerging markets have shown in part their potential. Particularly in the first ten years of the 1990s, the emerging securities markets will play a more and more important role in economic growth.

3. Various Restrictive Factors for Securities Investment in the Emerging Markets.

Despite the fact that emerging markets have provided favorable conditions for foreign investors, the growth has not been as rapid as expected. The reasons are multi-faceted. For instance, the legislation of investor nations sometimes set limits for the range of investment, such as not allowing pension funds and insurance companies to invest in foreign securities; some countries implement a foreign exchange control system. All these have reduced their opportunities to make investment overseas.

The two largest obstacles, however, are: International investors not having sufficient understanding of emerging securities markets; and developing countries not fully realizing the importance of foreign investments in securities, considering it a rare means of raising capital as compared with direct investment. Over the past decade or so, the impact of these two obstacles has been greatly mitigated, although they still constitute a component in the numerous obstacles still existing in many developing countries. Apart from the requirements of political stability and an overall sound economic environment, other more serious restrictive factors can be summed up as follows:

Liquidity: Generally speaking, the liquidity in emerging markets is insufficient, because bulky deals in shares often result in substantial price fluctuations in these markets. In the world, there are only about 100 non-American shares which are thought to be easily circulated. In certain sense, this situation is advantageous to foreign investors, because the limits in market liquidity can reduce the losses to their shares caused by stock market crashes.

Market Instability: Due to inflation and short trading caused by insufficient information about the companies as well as other factors, most emerging markets are relatively unstable. But, studies indicate that investing in these markets is not as risky for corporate investors as is popularly believed.

Investment Restrictions and Taxes: Some developing markets indiscriminately impose certain forms of investment restrictions upon and adopt tax regulations for foreign securities investors. The more typical include: Restrictions on the purchases of domestic shares by foreign or temporary residents (excluding direct investors) and control over transactions of foreign securities investments, particularly the control over the remittance of funds back to the investors' native countries (such as in Brazil); restrictions on the types of shares that can be bought by foreign securities investors, including the grades of shares, industries and enterprises or the percentages of shares to be held by foreign investors (such as in Mexico), and stipulations regarding the minimum span of time in which the foreign investments in securities cannot be cleared (such as in Chile). In terms of taxation, individual withholding tax and capital value-added tax rates of these countries have already become very close to international standards and will possibly be on par with them soon. But, some countries have replaced taxes on corporate income with withholding tax on dividends. This no doubt has produced an inhibiting impact on foreign investments in securities.

Complicated Regulations and Inefficient Operation Procedures: The regulation and operation systems of many emerging markets are underdeveloped, and this makes it hard to avoid complicated and inefficient registration, clearance and payment procedures. In quite a few countries, these procedures have been greatly simplified and systematized. Yet, there are still some problems waiting to be addressed.

Inadequate Investor Service and Security: Circulation of enterprise information and protection of investors are inadequate; the mode of account settlement in most emerging markets falls short of the practical needs of international business; and their means to punish insider trading is not well established.

Political Risks: In most emerging markets, political risks cannot be totally ignored. Nevertheless, it is not necessary to get as excited as in the past. One point that should be pointed out is that large transnational corporations operating in these countries are confronted with the same risks. Therefore, for those investors who usually put small amounts of money in emerging markets, the risks are not as serious as for those investors who invest in transnational corporations. In some situations, investors can underwrite property insurance policies with either official or private insurance companies.

4. Internationalization of Emerging Markets.

Three factors should be noted regarding internationalization of the emerging securities markets:

First, international corporate investors have shown great interest in emerging markets.

Second, large enterprises of some relatively developed countries have become unsatisfied with their domestic markets.

Third, emerging markets and the international market have entered an era of high information technology.

In addition, as a major healthy force for economic growth, political development worldwide prefers more liberal policies and freer markets, and greater attention is devoted to open economies and private enterprises. Most countries are clearly aware that they must base their economic development on the global market, rather than accomplish it by independent efforts. Their own national currencies and capital markets can develop only by being put into the international financial system and adapting them to the requirements of that system.

The internationalization of the emerging markets has the following four basic advantages:

1) An expanded domestic stock market strengthens the domestic economy.

2) Overseas investment in securities maintains economic growth, yet it does not substantially influence governmental control over the economy.

3) Thanks to the participation of overseas investors, investment banks and brokerage companies, domestic markets can quickly raise their efficiency, accumulate experience and mature.

4) Some companies in developing countries can first issue debt bonds, then turn these bonds into convertible securities and finally convert them into listed shares. In this way, they can gain access to the international market, and the amount of funds raised this way as well as the costs of raising capital are unmatched by domestic markets.

Of course, it is necessary to pay attention to the risks connected with internationalization, that is, the risks of unexpected inflow and outflow of active capital and the risks of loss of control over domestic companies. In practice, the risks are not as serious as some people envision. Both worries over the withdrawal of domestic funds and the outflow of foreign capital are indications of lack of confidence in the domestic economy. The more a country trys to use regulations to avoid competition in the world marketplace, the more its middle class tries to find ways to get around those restrictions and shelter its property outside the country. On the contrary, although the open policy may have short-term risks, it can effectively reduce the withdrawal of funds and absorb as well as keep foreign investments. With regard to company control, it is necessary to understand that the reason foreign investors invest in securities is to reap maximum returns at the minimum risks. Their aim is not to gain control over the companies they invest in.

5. Necessary Conditions for the Development of the Domestic Securities Market.

If a government wants to make its country's domestic market part of the international market, it must pay attention to reaching certain standards and always keep in touch with the international market.

This means developing countries must create the proper conditions by doing the following:

— Open up the market for foreign investment and trading to allow capital inflow and outflow.

— Deal with incomes from different kinds of financial securities with fair and identical financial means (particularly financial securities from which dividends are received and those upon which capital accumulation withholding tax is levied).

— Establish appropriate standard protective measures for investors.

— Establish in the market the technical standards and procedures required of securities, such as advanced laws and regulations, particularly laws concerning the capital market.

— Establish a committee which is sufficiently staffed and has ample funding and considerable power.

— Establish a dynamic, sufficiently transparent, rationally managed and highly efficient stock exchange, and make sure there are enough investors.

— Adopt accounting standards, financial prospectus and analytical methods that are conventionally used in the world.

— Enact ample securities settlement standards and procedures, and establish modern telecommunications networks.

Monetary institutions that are conducive to the development

of securities markets should also be established, such as credit rating institutions and a central custody system. Most important of all, there must be corporate investors, such as pension funds, life insurance companies and mutual funds.

Section 3 Improvement and Perfection of China's B-Shares Market

1. Issuance of B Shares in China — an Indication that China's Capital Market Has Been Incorporated into the International Capital Market.

Since December 1991, Shanghai and Shenzhen have issued to overseas investors renminbi special shares (B shares for short), raising some US$ 500 million and 730 million Hong Kong dollars respectively. This has opened up a new channel to absorb foreign funds and has served as a prelude to the internationalization of China's securities market, and thus is of great theoretical and practical significance.

(1) Viewed from the angle of domestic enterprises that have issued B shares, in addition to establishing much-needed new capital-raising channels and accomplishing the goal of absorbing long-term fixed foreign funds, it has also strengthened the links between domestic enterprises and the international capital market while increasing the efficiency of the enterprise operations. Enterprises that have issued B shares have had the opportunity to learn international standards of production and management from their interaction with foreign investors, enterprises and advisors.

(2) From the angle of overseas investors, the domestic market for B shares not only has satisfied their wish to invest in China's economic construction but also mitigated their risks in investing in China and enabled them to share in the benefits of the country's economic growth. Moreover, since stocks can be readily sold, it has provided a viable investment option for investors desiring liquidity.

(3) Looking from the angle of China's stock market as a

whole, when the B shares are issued and listed, their quotations are announced in more than 150 countries and regions throughout the world, resulting in the establishment of organic links between China's stock market and the stock markets of the world. The effect of this is that China's stock market no longer operates in seclusion. In addition, it also demonstrates that it has only taken a few years for China's stock market to develop into a market system equipped with fairly comprehensive legal and management systems as well as relatively smooth operation mechanisms. The fact that Shanghai and Shenzhen stock exchanges have successfully issued and listed B shares, with the participation of international investment personages, has laid a sound foundation for the future establishment of a wide-ranged internationalized capital market in China that attracts transnational consortiums, banks and enterprises.

(4) Viewed from the perspective of the entire securities business of the country, because of the opening of the B-shares market, richly experienced overseas transnational securities dealers have come to China to directly cooperate with Chinese securities dealers in the issuing and trading of China's B shares. Through this cooperation, domestic securities dealers have acquired top-notch stock market management experience from their overseas counterparts. Also, through competition with other dealers in the domestic market, China's domestic securities dealers can further raise China's level of securities issuing and trading.

2. Invigorating China's Dull B-Shares Market.

Judging by the performance of the B shares since its listing, the secondary market for B shares has been cold-shouldered by overseas investors, particularly so when compared with the vigorous market for A shares. In Shenzhen, the total volume of deals for a day has been only 20-30 million yuan at the best (normally just more than 10 million yuan). There have even been some days in which no deals are made at all. The B shares business at the Shanghai Stock Exchange is even duller; slack business in B shares has caused a downward trend in stock price. Why have these good-quality B shares given performed so poorly so shortly after being listed?

The major reasons are as follows:

(1) Incompleteness of the legal system regarding B shares. Now, only local provisions are taken as the legal foundation for transactions in B shares in Shenzhen and Shanghai; national laws and regulations concerning securities are still absent. Therefore, overseas investors are very careful about investing in B shares. This is the fundamental reason why B shares have failed to arouse their enthusiasm. Overseas investors hold that investment in shares is highly risky, even more so when investing in a stock market where there is not a comprehensive legal system. Therefore, until relevant laws and regulations are enacted, it is improbable that overseas investors will flock in large numbers to the secondary market for B shares.

(2) Difference in accounting standards. When overseas investors evaluate the achievements and efficiency of a listed company, they do it by internationally accepted standards. The accounting standards used by companies that were listed in the past were mainly those promulgated by China's Ministry of Finance. These accounting systems and rules were mostly established on the basis of the state ownership of property and the planned economy; they are different in certain aspects than internationally accepted standards. These differences are as follows: The exchange rate used by enterprises in accounting is divorced from the actual value of foreign exchanges; and the loss from bad debts, the depreciation and re-evaluation of fixed assets and some other aspects in accounting are irrational, leading to differences in the enterprises' operation costs as well as returns. As a result, when Chinese companies used this accounting system, overseas investors found it difficult to appraise the value of the company they were interested in, hence their interest was muffled.

(3) The operational procedures for the buying and selling of B shares are not canonical, the transaction costs are too high and there is an inherent exchange rate risk that comes with investment in B shares. Looking at the performance of Shenzhen's five

securities firms chartered to deal with the buying and selling of B shares, it is hard for overseas investors to understand the operational procedures, particularly the procedure to have funds remitted into China. This is because each of the five firms has its own operational procedures. For instance, while one or two of the firms stipulate that the minimum amount of money to open an account must be over 200,000 HK dollars, the others do not have this requirement; while some of the firms that do business in B shares on commission open fund collection and payment accounts in foreign exchange clearing banks in China, the others open the accounts in banks abroad. In addition, the commission for deals in B shares is higher, exceeding 1.05 percent in Shenzhen, to which an extra 0.1 percent is added if a chartered agent overseas is commissioned to handle the purchases and sales.

(4) Overseas investors, securities dealers and relevant banks lack understanding of the secondary market for China's B shares. Since the listing of the B shares, many overseas investors have inquired about the official procedures needed to buy and sell B shares. But when they followed the prescribed procedures and went to have their funds remitted, some banks in Hong Kong (not clearing banks) did not understand the procedures and refused to handle the remittances. Some investors brought bills of exchange into China and turned them to the securities dealers to have them collected; the securities dealers refused to accept the bills because they were not familiar with the settlement of foreign exchange accounts. All these have thrown cold water on investors' enthusiasm.

In view of the above reasons, it is necessary to adopt the following steps to invigorate the secondary market for China's B shares:

(1) Strengthening legislative work related to the securities market. The securities legal system is a prerequisite for stabilizing and expanding the securities market. Overseas investors, in particular, put higher demands on the legal system. To invigorate the market for B shares and continuously expand the B shares primary (issuance) market and secondary (trading) market in the future, it is necessary to enact as soon as possible the *Securities*

Law and other laws and regulations concerning the securities market, so as to further enhance the confidence of overseas investors in China's B shares.

(2) Reforming current accounting principles for listed companies and establishing new accounting principles that are as close as possible to internationally accepted principles and conventions. Now, the reform of China's accounting system should begin with adopting the accelerated depreciation method, the historical cost and market price offset methods and the method of setting aside reserves to offset bad debts. At the same time, it is necessary to improve the foreign exchange accounts of enterprises and keep accounts according to exchange rates that reflect the current value of foreign currencies. It is also necessary to improve the credit ranking of the companies that issue B shares and prepare relevant, open financial documents in accordance with international conventions, so as to give overseas investors a comprehensive and accurate financial background and enable them to make investment decisions accordingly.

(3) Standardizing and simplifying the buying and selling procedures and improving the operational system in the B shares marketplace. This includes the establishment of a bank system and an independent B-shares trading system and the separation of the trading system for B shares from the current computerized automated exchange system so as to guarantee the efficiency in the trading of B shares; the installation of international telecommunication facilities in the trading ring and special screen for demonstrating quotations of B shares; posting B-share prices in US dollars instead of renminbi; the improvement of the settlement and transfer of B shares, and making plans to establish China's B shares centralized settlement service in internationalized regions to handle in a unified manner the payment and collection of funds as well as the transfer and custody of shares after deals are concluded.

(4) Improving the expertise of securities dealers chartered to handle deals in B shares. In this respect, it should start with improving securities dealers' professional skill in handling foreign exchange business and their general knowledge of the securities

market.

(5) Strengthening publicity of B shares. Since overseas investors, securities dealers and banks lack full understanding of the operation of China's B shares secondary market, the departments concerned should improve their publicity of the market, including educating investors about the advantages of the B-shares market. This will encourage more investment.

(6) Expanding the scale of issuance and giving approval to a number of large companies to issue B shares with relatively larger nominal value so as to enhance their appeal to overseas major investors and mutual fund companies; and at the same time improving the liquidity of the B-shares market. At present, B shares are mostly issued to professional investors. As a result, the shares do not change hands frequently and the market exchange is not active. So, it is necessary to adopt measures to allow B shares to be directly listed on Hong Kong and foreign stock exchanges. At the same time, overseas securities dealers should be allowed to become overseas members of the Shenzhen Stock Exchange to directly accept commissions by overseas investors and they should be allowed to make deals on the stock exchange by telephone. This can not only enlarge the scope of B-share issuing, but also make it convenient for overseas individual investors to invigorate the B-shares market.

(7) Changing the form of pricing from renminbi to HK or US dollars to help investors to steer clear of currency exchange risks. Studies are already under way to solve this problem.

Apart from the issuance of B shares, other new channels should be explored for the internationalization of China's securities market, such as issuing China (Shenzhen) Securities Fund in Hong Kong or foreign countries, to indirectly absorb foreign funds into the Shenzhen and other securities markets in the hinterland of China; and selecting domestic enterprises with the necessary conditions to issue shares and deal in the stock markets in Hong Kong, Singapore, the United States as well as other countries and regions, so as to expand the vista in importing foreign funds via the stock market.

3. The Feasibility of Issuing B Shares Within China.

In order to bolster the issuing of B shares and increase the total volume of transactions in B shares, it is necessary to improve the issuance and circulation of B shares, and open the B-shares market to people within China's mainland who have foreign exchange. This would form a B-shares market that combines business overseas with business inside the country.

Opening the B-shares market and promoting their issuance and circulation within China is, both at present and in the long run, a move that benefits the country and the people. Its necessity is reflected in three aspects:

(1) The need to pool foreign exchange funds and open new fund-raising channels.

Opening new fund-raising channels and extensively absorbing and utilizing foreign funds are strategic policies China has adopted in the 1990s to expand the scope of reform and opening to the outside world, as well as for accelerating the pace of economic construction. The securities market, as one of the most effective means of raising foreign funds, will play a more and more important role. Recent experience has born this out: In over a year's time, China has attracted some US$ 600 million in foreign funds through the securities market; this has added an extra channel for raising foreign funds, enhanced China's prestige in the world and enabled the country to accumulate valuable experience in the operation of its securities market. It has played a positive role in promoting the development of China's securities market, amplifying enterprises' capacity to adapt to changes and development, in improving the domestic investment environment and increasing foreign exchange. Therefore, to pool idle foreign exchange resources within the country through domestic issuance and circulation of B shares will inevitably become a useful supplement to China's efforts in raising and utilizing foreign funds; at the same time, it is also an important way of improving and developing China's B shares market.

(2) The need to invigorate the circulation of securities and strengthen the vitality of enterprises.

In terms of the intrinsic relations and systematic functions of the securities market, issuing shares is the precondition for the circulation of securities; without an issue market of considerable scale, the circulation market will lack vigor; if the circulation market lacks vigor, securities will not be able to effectively play their role in raising funds, improving the efficiency and management of the enterprises, adjusting the composition of property right, optimizing industrial setup and promoting economic growth.

Generally speaking, China's B shares market is robust and fruitful. Yet, there are many drawbacks, the most conspicuous of which is the great gap between the circulation market and the issue market, market depression and a dearth of deals. To improve this situation, one important means is to allow B shares to be issued and circulated within the country to attract residents in the country with foreign exchange to the B-shares market. This can expand the scope of the market and invigorate securities circulation. The formation and development of the B-shares market within the country will eventually embark on the course towards the unification of markets both in and outside the country, which will inevitably cause corresponding changes in the mechanisms of domestic finance, planning, investment, banking and enterprise management. For those enterprises that issue B shares, both the external pressure and internal motivation will greatly increase, compelling them to pay more attention to the rational distribution of resources, the improvement of economic returns and the constant enhancement of their vitality — all of which will further accelerate the development of China's securities market.

(3) The need to maintain monetary order and correctly guide and protect investors' investment.

The stability and sound development of the securities market is directly related to the country's monetary order, the personal interests of the people and social stability. Thanks to the constant deepening of the economic restructuring and expansion of the scope of opening to the outside world over the past decade or more, China's economy has witnessed rapid, steady and coordinated development and the amount of foreign exchange in the hands of the people has increased by a wide margin. Nevertheless, the phenomenon of illegal trade of foreign exchange has also quietly developed. In some coastal areas, a few underground monetary organizations collaborated with overseas businessmen to engage in illegal deals of foreign exchange futures to defraud people of money, thus bringing great harm to the prestige of the renminbi as well as the interests of the general public, and disrupting the normal economic and monetary order. One of the reasons is that the singular channel for investment cannot meet the investment need of those people with foreign exchange. Therefore, allowing Chinese citizens who have foreign exchange in the country to directly participate the B-shares market not only provides them with a new channel for making investment but is also conducive to cracking down on law-breaking activities, stabilizing monetary order and promoting the sound development of the securities market.

Now, the opportunity and conditions have ripened for issuing B shares within the country, as manifested in these three aspects:

(1) Within China, people hold large amounts of foreign exchange.

Take the HK dollar for example. As the economic and trade relations between Hong Kong and the mainland of China have become closer and closer, the amount of HK dollar in circulation in southern China has become greater and greater. According to non-official statistics, the inflow accounts for 25-30 percent of the total issue in Hong Kong, that is, 14-17 billion HK dollars. According to statistics provided by the Bank of China, up to the end of 1992 China's private foreign exchange savings deposits were valued at about US$8 billion. But, as the interest rates for foreign exchange savings deposits were very low, the amounts of such deposits tended to go down in some coastal areas. In addition, there were very few places where foreign exchange can be used. Under such a situation, to open the B-shares market to people having foreign exchange not only can pool large amounts of idle foreign exchange scattered in society for investment and change its direction of flow, but also create a better opportunity for further inflow of funds in foreign exchange.

(2) In respect to the issuance and circulation of B shares, the domestic securities market has acquired a fairly sound foundation in terms of trained personnel and necessary experience; this experience extends to the international market as well.

With regard to the issue market, all the underwriters for B shares are famous securities dealers selected solely through intense competition. For instance, the 14 underwriters in Shenzhen include ones funded by British, French, American as well as Chinese investment. The cooperation between Chinese and foreign securities dealers has both ensured the success of the issues and enabled Chinese securities dealers to gain much valuable experience.

As for the circulation market, the buying and selling of B shares are directly handled by domestic securities dealers in Shanghai, while in Shenzhen they are handled by Chinese dealers when contacted by foreign dealers, or by Chinese dealers under direct commission from overseas investors. Through either direct or indirect deals, domestic securities dealers have learned something about basic operations, established closer links with overseas dealers and the B-shares clearing banks, and entered into closer cooperation with domestic accounting and law firms — all has enabled the performance of the B-shares market to approach the requirements of international conventions.

The pace of setting up new securities institutions has also been accelerated. Now, in China there are several dozen securities companies, including several major national ones, such as Nanfang, Guotai and Huaxia. The establishment and operation of major national securities companies has both greatly sped up the pace of building a national unified securities market and opened a broader vista for the internationalization of China's securities market.

(3) A sound foundation has been laid for legislative work concerning the B-shares market.

In succession, Shanghai has promulgated *Provisions Regarding the Management of Renminbi Special Shares of the Shanghai Municipality, Supplementary Regulations Regarding Trad-*

ing Market Transactions (Renminbi Special Shares) at the Shanghai Stock Exchange, and *Provisional Regulations Regarding Trustship Concerning B Shares at the Shanghai Stock Exchange.* Shenzhen also has promulgated *Provisional Regulations Regarding the Management of Renminbi Special Shares of Shenzhen City, Detailed Rules on the Implementation of the Provisional Regulations Regarding the Management of Renminbi Special Shares of Shenzhen City, Provisional Rules Regarding the Registration of Renminbi Special Shares of Shenzhen City,* and *Rules for Trading and Clearing Affairs of B Shares at the Shenzhen Stock Exchange.* All these rules and regulations have fairly comprehensively reflected the requirements for management of the B-shares market and will provide the basic legal conditions for the issuance and circulation of B shares on China's mainland. Of course, they still need to be further improved.

4. Propositions for the Improvement and Development of China's B-Shares Market.

There are two models to choose from for issuing and circulating B shares within China's mainland. One is closed operation, that is, to establish an independent B-shares market in the country; and the other is open operation, that is, to form an internal-external unified B-shares market. Judging by the current progress in the reform of China's monetary system, particularly the introduction of the shareholding system, as well as those dealing with the B-shares market, it is necessary to take an active yet steady attitude towards the issuance and circulation of B shares within the country; it is imperative both to take into consideration its importance and practical significance and to pay attention to the gradual nature of its development. Therefore, the overall strategy should be to gradually develop it, first adopting the closed operation model to establish the foundation and achieve experience, and then shifting to an open operation model when the time is right.

(1) Major Concepts of the Closed Operation Model

The Issue Market 1) Select some experimental shareholding enterprises in the economically developed or relatively developed regions to issue B shares, which are sold to people having foreign exchange within the country. The B-shares issuing enterprises can issue A shares at the same time, but cannot issue B shares abroad. 2) The shares can be issued at the nominal value or at a premium; usually, the price of B shares should be fixed according to the average price level on the overseas markets; and the issue prices should be determined based on each enterprise's assets, debts and efficiency. 3) The form of issuance should be open and socialized; local citizens and citizens in other places should be given equal rights to buy, and securities dealers should have wide representation so that the principle of being open, equal and fair and transparency of the market can be maintained. 4) Currencies that can be used to buy B shares should not be limited and the payment can be in any freely convertible foreign currency, such as the US dollar, the HK dollar, the Japanese yen or the Deutch mark. However, in order to avoid confusion, particularly the risks caused by changes in exchange rates to issuing companies, one currency, probably the US dollar, should be taken as the base by which the value of other currencies is calculated (following current exchange rates on the world money market). The risks and losses caused by changing exchange rates during the course of transactions should be borne by the investors themselves.

The Circulation Market 1) All transactions in B shares must be conducted through floor trading and no over-the-counter black market deals are allowed. The trading places should be the Shanghai and Shenzhen stock exchanges. Considerations can be made to open a special stock exchange in Beijing or Tianjin for B shares (which can be gradually expanded into a unified B-shares exchange for both domestic and overseas deals or a comprehensive stock exchange), thus forming a north-south balanced B-shares issuance and circulation network. 2) The forms of quotation should be unified — it would be best to make them in US dollars. The same should be applied to clearing as well as delivery. 3) In line with the amount of foreign currency in the hands of the individual citizens, it is appropriate to set the amount of shares for one deal at 100 or 50, while treating a deal less than the set amount as odd-lot shares. 4) The transaction, clearing and delivery of B shares within the country can adopt current practices. Also efforts should be made to quickly establish B-shares clearing houses jointly funded by stock exchanges, securities registration companies and clearing banks and participated in by related securities dealers. This will shorten the time span for clearing and improve the efficiency of transactions. 5) The standards of transaction fees should be the same as for A shares. 6) An independent comprehensive index that reflects the performance of trading in B shares within the country should be worked out. At the same time, to avoid creating any unnecessary confusion, a new name may be chosen for it.

Market Regulation It is necessary to establish a regulatory mechanism that is based on indirect regulation and combines government planning and market forces. 1) Developing market mechanisms, mainly by unifying the supply and demand mechanism, competition mechanism and transaction mechanism between different securities markets will enable macroeconomic regulation to produce a balanced effect between the securities markets. 2) Developing indirect regulatory means, mainly by establishing a stabilization fund. The sources of the fund should be: A part from the securities issuance costs (which can be considered when shares are issued at a premium); a part from securities transaction fees, and a part from the state's foreign exchange funds. The scale of the fund can be decided in line with the scale of the market; it can play a certain stabilizing and guiding role when sharp fluctuations appear in market prices. 3) Developing flexible planned regulatory means; guidance plans should primarily aim at short-term goals of securities market development and they can be flexibly adjusted in line with practical needs to give full expression to market forces. 4) The control by the state over the securities market shuld mainly be through policies and laws; it is necessary to enforce the state's authority in market regulation and improve regulatory efficiency. 5) Strictly enforcing market supervision and management to prevent defraud and cheating.

(2) Major Concepts of the Open Operation Model

When the basic conditions are ripened for the domestic B-shares market to move from the closed operation stage to the open operation stage, the issuance and circulation of both the domestic and overseas B-shares market can be brought together to form a unified market. In order to ensure stable performance and sound development of the unified market, it is imperative to make necessary alterations in accordance with the demands of the international conventions and China's realities. Major attention should be devoted to the following:

The Issue Market 1) Gearing both expanded issues and new issues towards individual citizens and professional groups at home and abroad; reasonably deciding the total amount of the issues as well as the proportions to be shared by the domestic and overseas markets. In principle, the amount for the overseas market should be more than that for the domestic market. 2) The form of issuance should be open. Under this prerequisite, the means to that end should be decided by both the domestic and overseas underwriters through consultation; yet their activities must be subject to the supervision of departments in charge of securities business. 3) Widening the scope and expanding the scale of the issues so as to enhance the prestige of China's securities market throughout the world.

The Circulation Market 1) Individual citizens and professional groups both at home and abroad should be able to freely buy or sell currently or previously issued B shares in the domestic and overseas markets; or they can commission securities dealers both at home and abroad to buy or sell on their behalf. The stipulations regarding direct or indirect commission trading must be abolished to protect investors' free choice. 2) Taking into account the current purchasing power of the Chinese general public by setting the amount of shares for one deal at 100-500. 3) The stock exchanges at different places will each establish a central clearing house and bring in overseas securities dealers through appropriate reform of the former clearing houses. 4) Unifying the standards of transaction fees to be collected and working out a unified comprehensive index for the B-shares market. 5) Making great efforts to improve the telecommunications facilities and means of operation.

Market Regulation 1) Improving the B-shares market regulatory mechanism which takes regulation by the market as the key; the government's wishes for macroeconomic regulation should be mainly realized through laws and regulations; attention should be paid to increasing the role of the stabilization fund, the scope of which should be expanded to include funds from overseas securities dealers. 2) Strengthening the guidance of plans as well as the construction of an information system. 3) Strengthening self-regulation of the securities business as well as social supervision: improving self-regulation and control by establishing necessary self-regulatory organizations and enacting necessary systems, and organically combining the overall control by the government with self-regulation by the securities business. This can be accomplished by bringing into active play the supervisory role of the securities administrative departments, accounting and law firms, auditing organizations and the general public. 4) Improving th credit rating and consultancy systems of the securities market as well as their functions by inviting personnel from overseas securities and banking businesses to take part; educating the public about how to reap better investment returns.

What needs to be pointed out here is that the securities business is an industry closely related to national economic system and policies. Therefore, either in the closed or open model operation, attention must be paid to the question of supporting reforms in the development of the B-shares market. Now, the focuses should be: Expanding the scope of experiment in the shareholding system and standardizing it; accelerating reforms in the monetary and foreign exchange systems, continuously strengthening and improving the securities market macro-regulation system and enhancing the regulatory means to bring about coordinated operation and a balanced cycle in both macro and micro terms; and renewing efforts in legislative work to promulgate and put into effect national laws and regulations concerning the securities market as well as laws and regulations specially designed for the B-shares market, so as to form a well-knit, orderly and mutually conditioning legal system. In addition, it is necessary to strengthen ideological work, professional ethics education in securities circles, and improve organization-building in the securities business. Furthermore, ways must be found to enhance the general public's knowledge about financial investment and its inherent risks.

To emphasize the transitional model of gradual development for the B-shares market does not means to slow down the pace of unification of the securities market as a whole. Rather, it is aimed at laying a solid foundation based on international conventions and China's realities. Also, by slowly building up professional experience, this method will create a solid foundation for the sustained, stable and coordinated development of China's B-shares market after the unification of the securities market.

Section 4 Obstacles and Countermeasures for Internationalization of China's Securities Market

1. Internationalization of China's Securities Market Is Conducive to Raising Funds and Standardizing Enterprise Management; Yet China's Underdeveloped Legal System and Market Mechanisms Impose Obstacles.

China's securities market reflects a global trend whereby the flow of international capital is increasing and accelerating. This capital is mainly in the form of securities. The governments and large enterprises of various countries as well as transnational corporations and international monetary organizations regard the international securities market as a regular channel for capital raising and investment. The rapid development of China's securities market put the question of its internationalization on the agenda before most people were aware of the issue.

(1) The internationalization of China's securities market is determined by the inherent demands of its economic development and the development of its stock market. China is a developing country and it is short of funds for economic construction. The shortage of funds can be partly solved by internal accumulation. Yet, it is still necessary to expand our efforts to absorb and utilize foreign funds. The securities market can be regarded as a good way to bring in foreign funds because it can guarantee that

enterprises raise much-needed funds without increasing the country's foreign debt burden.

(2) The internationalization of China's securities market is based on the need to push domestic enterprises to the international market. Through the issuance and listing of shares, domestic enterprises can get involved with and become better known in the international market. They can also learn the operation principles of the international market and enhance their competitive edge there. Internationalization is an inherent demand of economic development and also represents the direction China's enterprises are moving in.

(3) The internationalization of China's securities market is a demand of the standardization of the country's stock market. Viewed from the perspective of stock market development, it is hard for a secluded stock market to survive in an open social and economic environment. To accomplish the internationalization of China's stock market in a timely manner, China must urgently develop a standard stock market; this will promote the self-improvement of the country's securities market as well as its growth.

(4) The internationalization of China's securities market can make efficient use of domestic surplus funds. Generally speaking, China has suffered a shortage of funds for a considerably long time. Yet, along with the development of the economy, it is not rare that some places and departments have fund surpluses. By incorporating China's stock market into the international stock market, these surplus funds will become international capital and will quickly circulate in the international monetary market seeking the best investors and capital-raisers throughout the world in order to reap maximum returns.

Moreover, the internationalization of China's securities market will also produce an active impact on changing the management mechanism of domestic enterprises, on the stability of the domestic securities market as well as on the efficient flow and distribution of the country's economic resources.

The internationalization of the securities market depends on certain conditions. China has not yet fully acquired these conditions. Therefore, there are still some obstacles for the internationalization of China's stock market.

First, China's securities market is not yet well developed, and this adversely affects its internationalization.

(1) There are some differences between China's accounting system and assets evaluation system and the conventional systems of the world, and this makes the appraised value of assets of the listed enterprises lose its credibility. As a result, most of the listed companies fall short of international standards for financial statements, assets evaluation and transparency, and fail to meet the requirements of overseas investors.

(2) Due to insufficient securities market legislation, the rights and obligations of investors, as well as the protection of their rights and interests, are not defined in clear-cut legal stipulations, making investors feel legally vulnerable.

(3) China's securities market lacks depth and width. This makes it difficult to establish new funds: a fund should have 20-30 varieties of shares in it so as to spread the risk around. Therefore, it is necessary to actively expand the scope of experimentation in the shareholding system, so as to increase the varieties of listed shares and widen the scope of the market.

(4) China's securities market has not provided investors with financial instruments to avoid risks. Judging by the experience of other countries, when a stock market develops to a certain stage, it requires a supporting futures market to help transfer risks. For some time, China's B-shares market has remained dull and lacked appeal. The most important reason is that overseas investors, if investing in the market, will shoulder great risks, while necessary financial instruments that can help them avoid risks are absent. Therefore, it is highly necessary to establish China's financial futures market to provide overseas investors with a financial instrument to avoid risks. First, it is necessary to make preparations to establish as soon as possible China's stock index futures market.

Second, services that are related to the securities market, such as assets evaluation and consultancy services, are relatively backward in their development, affecting both the operational efficiency of the stock market and the internationalization of China's securities market.

2. Measures for Internationalization of China's Securities Market.

Judging by the experience of Japan and the Republic of Korea, the internationalization of a country's securities market is closely linked to its economic development and economic strength; it cannot be accomplished simply by the will of people. Viewed from the perspective of China's realities, the internationalization of China's securities market cannot possibly be accomplished at one stroke; it should follow the law of economic development and develop gradually. Specifically speaking, it should go through the following stages of development:

(1) The stage of indirect participation. It is necessary to look at the experience of Japan, the Republic of Korea and Taiwan at the initial stage of their securities market internationalization. At this stage, overseas investors made indirect investments in China's stock market through funds either managed by Chinese securities companies, or by foreign securities companies, or by trust and investment corporations jointly established by Chinese and foreign monetary organizations. To adopt this form at the initial stage of internationalization has the following advantages: First, this form of indirect investment will be welcomed by the investors because it produces greater returns, has lower risks and allows greater fluidity. Second, it can by-pass geographical limits and overcome the obstacles resulting from different trading systems, conventions and foreign exchange control systems of various countries to meet the different needs of investors at different strata. And finally, fund investment can hold appeal for more individual investors wishing to pool together small sums of money and turn short-term investments into long-term investments. Moreover, fund investment can effectively combat the unlawful market manipulating activities of major securities buyers and sellers and hold in check gambling and speculation, so as to effect a comparatively smooth transition of China's stock market towards the international stock market.

(2) The initial phase of the stage of direct participation. It is necessary, in line with China's demand for funds as well as the development of the domestic stock market, to adopt various policies which promote the inflow of overseas capital, limit the outflow of domestic funds and open the stock market (within limits).

First, it is necessary to allow Chinese enterprises to issue stocks and convertible bonds overseas and allow overseas securities companies to establish offices in the country to conduct securities investment activities, and to speed up securities capital export activities in a planned way. Second, it is necessary, on the one hand, to allow Chinese securities companies to set up offices or branch companies abroad to collect information and encourage overseas investors to invest in China; and on the other, to provide Chinese investors with investment services in foreign markets. Finally, it is necessary to gradually allow Chinese enterprises to list on major overseas stock exchanges. In view of China's specific conditions, Hong Kong should be considered a major channel for China to absorb foreign funds. At present, efforts should be made to increase the number of enterprises listed on the Hong Kong stock exchange.

(3) The later phase of the stage of direct participation. By then, the internationalization of China's securities market will have reached a high degree, economic policies will have become more relaxed and the domestic stock market will have been further improved. Moreover, the greatly increased economic strength of the country will make it possible to turn idle funds in society into capital. Then, it will be possible to accelerate the internationalization of China's securities market. First, the scope of overseas funds and the intermediary for overseas investors to invest in China's stock market can be expanded; so can the amount and scope of shares and convertible bonds issued abroad by Chinese enterprises. Also, foreign securities companies can be allowed to set up branch companies or new securities companies in China, or put new capital in Chinese securities companies. At the same time, the limits on the outflow of domestic funds should be gradually removed, and domestic individual investors and

investment organizations can be allowed to invest in overseas shares; and foreign enterprises will be allowed to list on China's stock exchanges. Only by allowing the free flow of international capital between China's stock market and the international stock market can it be possible to really incorporate China's stock market into the international stock market.

The above-discussed stages are only rough sketches. It is impossible to draw strict demarcation lines between them. The internationalization of China's securities market still calls for massive and meticulous work — corresponding supporting management policies as well as laws and regulations should be enacted for each stage to guide the progress of internationalization. The time limit for various places cannot possibly be precisely stated. For instance, it has taken Taiwan only 10 years to realize the internationalization of its stock market (from the early 1980s to the present); it took the Republic of Korea around 15 years (from the early 1980s to the first half of 1990s); and it took Japan a longer time (from the late 1950s to the mid-1970s). The situation on China's mainland is somewhat different from them. In the very early stages of its securities market development, China started working to promote its internationalization. Moreover, as the economic environment of the world changes quickly, it is impossible for China to mechanically copy others' methods. But, there is a lesson China should learn from them: To be a successful player in the international securities market, it is necessary to first foster a healthy and strong domestic securities market.

图书在版编目(CIP)数据

中国的证券市场:英文/高尚全,迟福林主编.
—北京:外文出版社,1996
ISBN 7 – 119 – 01491 – 9

Ⅰ.中… Ⅱ.①高… ②迟… Ⅲ.证券交易 – 金融市场
– 中国 – 英文 Ⅳ.F832.5

中国版本图书馆 CIP 数据核字 (95) 第 23585 号

中国的证券市场

高尚全   迟福林   主编

*

ⓒ外文出版社

外文出版社出版

(中国北京百万庄路 24 号)

邮政编码 100037

北京外文印刷厂印刷

中国国际图书贸易总公司发行

(中国北京车公庄西路 35 号)

北京邮政信箱第 399 号   邮政编码 100044

1996 年(大 32 开)第一版

(英)

ISBN 7 – 119 – 01491 – 9 /F·33(外)

02250

4 – E – 3081P